ritain
1815-1867

C000318930

Edited by

Peter Catterall

Heinemann Educational
a division of Heinemann Publishers (Oxford) Ltd.
Halley Court, Jordan Hill, Oxford OX2 8EJ

OXFORD   LONDON   EDINBURGH
MELBOURNE   MADRID   ATHENS
BOLOGNA   PARIS   SYDNEY
AUCKLAND   SINGAPORE   TOKYO
IBADAN   NAIROBI   HARARE
GABORONE   PORTSMOUTH NH (USA)

First published 1994

British Library Cataloguing in Publication Data

A catalogue record for this book is available from the British Library

ISBN 0 435 31000 3

Printed and bound in Great Britain by Clays Ltd, St Ives plc.

Front cover *The Peterloo Massacre* by George Cruikshank
(Bridgeman Art Library).

Acknowledgements

Heinemann and the ICBH wish to thank all the contributors who have
given permission for their works to be published in this book.

Contents

Introduction

The French wars which ended with Wellington's victory at Waterloo in 1815 provided further stimulus for Britain's gradual industrialisation. The war created demand for the products of the metal-working industries, already growing as a result of technological innovations since the middle of the eighteenth century. It also encouraged the growth of the new textile industry.

Apart from these two industries the process of industrialisation remained patchy and incomplete . The largest group of workers were still the agricultural labourers. Indeed, in the 1820s and 1830s their numbers were still growing. This was an important backdrop to the 'Captain Swing' disturbances in the rural South in the early 1830s, sparked by attempts to introduce labour-saving machinery at a time of widespread underemployment on the land, compounded by the effect of the enclosures of the late eighteenth and early nineteenth centuries.

The effects of war and the advent of the machine also encouraged distress and social conflict elsewhere. Population growth was even more rapid in the towns than on the land. Grain production did not keep pace. Wartime shortages and bad harvests pushed bread prices to a succession of new heights, peaking in 1813. With memories of this still fresh, the renewal of the Corn Laws, in 1815, by a Parliament in which the landed interest was dominant was a major stimulus for the reform movement of the immediate post-war period. At the same time wage reductions for the skilled workers, increasingly being replaced by the mechanisation of production, led to the machine-breaking associated with Luddism. The resultant distress was compounded by high taxation to help fund the war effort.

These discontents were felt to originate with, and require the reformation of, a corrupt and oppressive state. For many of the defenders of the existing system the British Constitution was, however, in no need of reform. The balance between Crown, Lords and Commons achieved after the 'Glorious Revolution' of 1688 was felt to preserve and ensure liberties and freedom from tyranny. Reform ran the risk of undermining Parliament from being the deliberative forum of the nation as represented by an informed, educated and disinterested (in their view) élite. It would, it was feared, destroy a system in which power and influence and the maintenance of social order rested upon possession of property rights, apprehensions enhanced by the example of the French Revolution. Parliament would meanwhile become an assembly at the mercy of self-interested outside 'opinion'.

Reform agitation and its attendant disorders were accordingly met with firm resistance. But at the same time there were attempts to relieve causes of discontent amongst those disparate, regionally and occupationally divided groups that were coming to be called the working classes. Ineffective attempts to suppress trade unions during the French Wars (1793–1815) contrasted with efforts to encourage the growth of friendly societies. Measures to control seditious or subversive activities in 1817 coincided with legislation to combat unemployment through public works programmes.

There was also an increasing sense amongst the dominant élites of a need to respond to the social dislocation caused by industrial and urban growth by not just relieving the distress of the working classes, but by integrating and improving them. Education, for instance, was a means of improving the morals and condition of the working classes. By 1811, both Nonconformists and Anglicans had established educational societies to set up schools. Education was also a means to improve social cohesion. The Mechanics' Institute movement which began in Scotland at the start of the century, often with the support of employers, claimed that the education it provided would strengthen 'the firmness of the bond which unites all orders of society'. By the 1830s the view that education could play this valuable integrative role was triumphing over fears that it would feed revolution by giving the working classes ideas above their station. Its provision began, after 1833, to enjoy increasing government support.

Other problems, such as the repeated cholera epidemics between 1831 and 1866, led to measures to improve towns where the working classes lived. The 'Old Corruption' of the state against which the reformers and Chartists railed, proved capable of reforming itself. The greatest symbol of this was the repeal of the Corn Laws in 1846. Economic distress was no less marked in the 1850s than the 1840s, indeed, real wage levels stagnated after steady improvements over the previous 30 years. Criticism of the state, however, declined dramatically. The working classes, instead of being threats to order, meanwhile became, through their friendly societies and co-operatives, increasingly respectable. However, there were still those who were apprehensive of enfranchising even the best of the working classes, fearing that it would replace disinterested government with government by and for a class for whom the vote was not a privilege of citizenship but something to be used and abused in pursuit of their own self-interest.

Britain successfully coped with major economic, demographic and social strains in the first half of the nineteenth century, adjusting by a process of modest administrative and constitutional reform. However smoothly the transition seems to have been managed in retrospect by governments whose authority was never seriously challenged, the risks at the time nevertheless felt real enough. It is important to recognise that for many the Second Reform Act in 1867 was genuinely, and in every sense, still very much a 'leap in the dark'.

PART I
Before Reform

The Pittite coalition ended the French wars in 1815 with high taxation and a huge National Debt. Liverpool's government aimed to tackle these problems and, at the same time, introduce tariff reductions and retain income-tax. Their defeat on this, in 1816, illustrates the continuing independence of many MPs in the unreformed Parliament. These country gentlemen usually supported the government of the day but, on this occasion, they were more concerned with protecting their own interests. Though opposed by Manchester millowners and London radicals Parliament, at their behest, reintroduced the Corn Laws in 1815.

This measure, coupled with an economic downturn and the continuing heavy burden of taxation, encouraged the rise of radical activity during 1815–19. Repression and surveillance were mingled with concessions. The main means of social control, however, remained the magistracy, dominated by the local landowning élite and Anglican clergy. They had proved adequate in the eighteenth century, but Peel concluded there was a need for a police force in the Metropolis. The Metropolitan Police Force was thus formed in 1829.

By 1829, the Pittite Tories were in decline. Public expenditure cuts had restored sound finance, whilst economic revival after 1821 allowed the reduction of some tariffs. These measures nevertheless remained suspect to many Tory supporters, and were blamed for the downturn that followed the banking crisis of 1825. The Government began to break up after Liverpool's retirement in 1827. The splits opened up with the appointment of Canning, a pro-Catholic emancipationist, in 1827. This episode institutionalised a rift between Canningites and Wellington's supporters. The Tory right were then alienated by the passage of Catholic emancipation in 1829.

The Whigs were finally given their opportunity by Wellington's rejection of reform the following year. Grey had first proposed reform in the 1790s and Whig interest was revived by the issue of corrupt boroughs such as Grampound. However, as late as 1827, the cause of reform seemed sufficiently hopeless for a number of Whigs to agree to serve in Canning's Government, despite his known opposition to reform. In 1830, in contrast, it was the Canningites who joined a Whig Government committed to reform.

Eric Evans
The Premiership of Lord Liverpool

Lord Liverpool's premiership was the longest in the nineteenth century. Eric Evans analyses why the Tory coalition he led stayed together for as long as it did.

Liverpool was Prime Minister during that time of massive transition and upheaval known as the Industrial Revolution. New textile towns, such as Bolton and Rochdale, were being created, and older towns, like Manchester and Leeds, utterly transformed. The population of Britain was growing rapidly and, to many contemporaries, alarmingly. When Liverpool took office, the population of Britain was about 12.25m. When he resigned, it had swollen by more than 20% to about 15m. Lord Liverpool, in fact, presided over the most rapid period of population growth in Britain's history – a factor which might be thought to lead to instability rather than stability in government.

Liverpool's qualities

Since very long-lived ministries are a great rarity in British politics, it is worth asking why this one lasted so long, especially during a time of such bewilderingly rapid change. The consensus among historians used to be that, whatever factors did explain it, high political quality was not among them. The famously unfair description – 'the Arch-Mediocrity' – penned by Benjamin Disraeli in his novel *Coningsby* (1844), stuck fast. Certainly, Liverpool was no intellectual giant. He had come into politics, like so many of his contemporaries, because of his family name. His father had been a leading adviser of George III who had been rewarded not only by political influence but by a hereditary title. Because of his privileged background, Liverpool was able to get into parliament young and he served a long political apprenticeship. In the 1790s, as Pitt's Commissioner at the Board of Control, he became especially knowledgeable about commercial matters. Since Pitt's own ministry was long and stable, Liverpool's career was not blighted by the downfall of his political mentor.

As a young politician, he was respected more than admired. His speeches were logical and detailed, but rarely inspiring. He was increasingly accused of being too fussy, too timid, and lacking a broad command of policy matters. Little about Liverpool marked him out as a future Prime Minister, let alone one who would stay in office for almost 15 years. Beyond a certain point, however, brainpower is probably more of a handicap than an advantage for a successful politician. The ability to think brilliantly original thoughts, for example, can be deeply unsettling both for their progenitor and his political colleagues. Consistency, dependability and the ability to compromise are more bankable assets, and Liverpool had all three. As Norman Gash's recent brief but impressive biography has shown,[1] Liverpool's ability to get the best out of colleagues, many of whom, like Canning and Peel, were abler than himself, was a priceless asset. His cabinet ministers trusted him; their private papers rarely, if ever, speak of their feeling let down by his leadership.

Liverpool was also an effective and sensitive chairman of Cabinet, an institution which was itself in the early stages of development. He trusted cabinet colleagues to run their departments and was rewarded by loyalty. His relations with George IV were not always so smooth. In November 1820, the new King, frustrated by Liverpool's evident mistrust of his judgement in seeking to divorce his wife, Queen Caroline, contemplated dismissing him. Liverpool was able to convince the King that no cabinet colleague would be able to form a stable ministry in his stead, and the King had to back down. The declining powers of, and respect for, the monarchy was a significant factor in Liverpool's long tenure of power. A more powerful and popular King than George IV would almost certainly have managed to secure Liverpool's dismissal, if his mind were set upon it. The growth of cabinet solidarity coincided with the decline of the monarchy as an independent factor in political life.

Particularly later in his ministry, it was clear that although the effective ministers Liverpool had appointed in the 1820s would work under his leadership, they would find it very difficult to work under anyone else. The true measure of Liverpool's understated and emollient leadership is gauged only by hindsight. Within five years of his resignation, the Tory Party over which he had presided for so long had all but broken up. Some ministers joined the Whigs and, in 1832, the Tory Party suffered their most humiliating election defeat yet. This is not to say that the Tories would have continued in effortless command had Liverpool not been struck down, but his resignation was a huge blow to the party.

Consolidating the ministry

Liverpool, then, had positive leadership qualities of a kind which are frequently undervalued. However, no one can hold supreme office for long periods in a country where mechanisms exist for the peaceful and orderly transfer of power without a good deal of luck. Luck undoubtedly helped Liverpool in the early years. He had not been the Prince Regent's choice as Prime Minister on Spencer Perceval's assassination in 1812 and his administration was decidedly unsure in its early months, when the price of wheat (the staple grain for bread) reached its highest point in the whole of the nineteenth century, and widespread discontent erupted, especially in the industrial north. Rivals hoped for a speedy collapse of the ministry and Liverpool was fortunate indeed that his most vulnerable years at home coincided with the final turn of the tide in the long wars against France which had been going on, almost without a break, since 1793. Wellington's victories, first in the Iberian peninsula and then, decisively, against Napoleon in June 1815, were most important in stabilising Liverpool's ministry.

Liverpool's career also benefited from a strong degree of consensus within the established political classes in Britain. Party allegiances were not so firm as they were to become later in the century but by the early years of the nineteenth century, in contrast to much of the eighteenth, the Whig and Tory parties were separately identifiable at Westminster, and most MPs owed allegiance to one or the other, rather than primarily to an aristocratic patron or 'borough owner'.[2] The French Revolution, the effects of which thoroughly alarmed princes and hereditary landowners throughout Europe in the generation after 1789, contributed significantly towards the reformulation of political ideology in Britain. The overwhelming majority of MPs were from privileged, usually landed, backgrounds and most of them saw the French Revolution as nothing less than a challenge to civilisation and order as they knew it.[3]

An important political realignment had taken place in Britain in 1794, when 'conservative' Whigs under the Duke of Portland had come into coalition with William Pitt's government, to provide a much larger majority for policies designed to preserve the old order against challenges from political reformers and other sympathisers with the French Revolution. In one form or another, this coalition, which it would not be inappropriate to call the 'new Tory Party', ruled Britain for all but a few months from 1794 to 1830.

Tory ideology at this time developed a degree of coherence and consistency not seen since the reign of Queen Anne (1702–14). Tory ideology rejected principles of representative government based on abstract 'rights' of citizenship and upheld property rights as more effective guarantors of stability, which had been much longer established. It defended the Church of England, and argued that all attacks on the Church were by definition attacking the state as well. Popular targets of Tory abuse were those alleged to be 'Jacobins and Atheists'. It upheld the rights of land over those of commerce when the two were in conflict, since land was the pre-eminent form of property. Liverpool tried, not always with success, to harmonise the interests of land and commerce. The imposition of a new Corn Law in 1815, for example, was widely interpreted by merchants and other commercial figures as a crude means of giving special protection for the landed interest from which Liverpool and the great majority of MPs sprang. It was noticeable that, during Liverpool's Prime Ministership, MPs with commercial or industrial wealth were much more likely to be Whig supporters, while the Tory Party was immensely popular with the smaller landowners and country squires.[4]

The Conservative coalition

All of this is crucial to understanding Liverpool's long period in office. Though he was insecure as Prime Minister in his first few years, the Tory Party he later headed remained the overwhelmingly dominant 'Conservative coalition' which Pitt and Portland had fashioned 20 years earlier. Fear of the spread of 'French principles', including republicanism, attacks on the Church and democratic representation, kept it together even after Napoleon's fall and the re-establishment of a monarchy in France.

The stability of Lord Liverpool's Prime Ministership depended critically on the fact that most MPs in the early nineteenth century had grown to political maturity in the shadow of the French Revolution, and continued to fear the ideas it had unleashed at least until the 1820s. Within Parliament, and among the propertied classes outside, the so-called repressive legislation of 1819, when radical disaffection was at its peak, was strongly supported. The fury it excited among radical journalists and intellectuals like Cobbett, Wade and Shelley was real enough and the government undoubtedly lost the propaganda war during the years of economic hardship. It needs to be remembered, however, that vituperation and satire, however diverting for future historians, rarely bring down governments, particularly those whose propertied power bases were, like Liverpool's by 1819, secure.

The calmer, and economically more prosperous, years of the 1820s strengthened Liverpool's position still more, since extra-parliamentary political agitation dwindled. To that prosperity the sound economic management and the reduction of tariffs associated with Robinson and Huskisson contributed something, although the massive economic upswing which followed the postwar depression owed relatively little to political factors.

Finally, Liverpool in the 1810s and 1820s faced a weak and divided opposition. The establishment of the 'Conservative coalition' in 1794 had gravely weakened the Whigs. Many of those who remained with the Whig Party under the leadership of Charles James Fox espoused the cause of parliamentary reform when that cause was widely condemned by property owners as certainly foolish and dangerous, and possibly even treasonable. After Fox's death in 1806, the Whig Party was led by Charles Grey, who had supported reform in the 1790s but who believed that the issue hampered the reunification of the Whigs.

Ideologically, the Whigs were less coherent than the Tories and, once Liverpool's ministry appeared firmly established after 1815, marginal supporters fell away and new splits emerged. The general elections of 1818 and 1826 brought the Whigs little or no comfort, confirming Liverpool's strong parliamentary position. In 1822, the supporters of Baron Grenville, who had been a Pittite, but had left the coalition in 1801 and had usually voted with the Whigs thereafter, threw in their lot with the government. Dispirited and demoralised, the Whigs offered little sustained or effective opposition to Liverpool in his last five years of office, despite the tempting opportunities afforded by growing Tory divisions about Catholic emancipation.

Liverpool's long period as Prime Minister, then, owes much to good fortune, both political and economic, and to weak opposition. We should not conclude, however, that he was merely lucky. Liverpool was an experienced, knowledgeable and effective politician with a great talent for emollient chairmanship and for getting intrinsically abler, if sometimes fractious, ministers to work harmoniously under his leadership. His virtues are hardly heroic, and not at all romantic. One can see why they did not appeal to Disraeli. Yet Disraeli's own judgements were far from unimpeachable, and it is high time that his misleading put-down was itself laid to rest.

Notes

(1) Gash, N. *Lord Liverpool* (Weidenfeld & Nicolson, 1984).
(2) O'Gorman, F. 'Party politics in the early nineteenth century, 1812–32' in *English Historical Review*, cii, 63–84.
(3) Evans, E. J. *Liberal Democracies* (Joint Matriculation Board, 1990) pp. 83–92.
(4) Evans, E. J. *Britain Before the Reform Act: Politics and Society, 1815–1832*, Seminar Studies in History (Longman, 1989).

Eric Evans is Professor of Social History at Lancaster University.

Wendy Hinde
George Canning 1770–1827:
A Career Blighted by Ambition?

George Canning was a crucially important political figure in the final decades of pre-Reform Britain, but one whose ambition frequently deprived him of office and the country of his services.

George Canning had a lengthy political career but, if one looks at it as a whole, it is striking to find how often he was his own worst enemy. For someone who became one of the most famous of British Foreign Secretaries, he spent a surprisingly large proportion of his political life in circumstances that did not allow him to develop his potential as a states-man. And with one important exception, it was not the ups and downs of politics or any factor outside his own control that held him back until the last five years of his life. It was his own faults of character and judge-ment, and it was only because of Castlereagh's tragic suicide that he finally got the opportunity which he turned to such good account.

Castlereagh's tragedy was Canning's good fortune. At the begin-ning of his life he was also fortunate. His father died when his son was only a year old, leaving his widow with so little money that she had to go on the stage, which was then a very disreputable thing to do. But when George was eight he was adopted by his uncle, Stratford Canning, a well-to-do-City merchant, who sent him to Eton and Oxford, where he not only received a good education but was able to make the social contacts which would greatly help him in pub-lic life. After Oxford, in 1791, he went to London to read for the Bar at Lincoln's Inn. Already a political career was his real goal, although he was not yet sure how he was going to get started and where he stood in politics. His uncle and aunt, the Stratford Cannings, were enthusiastic Whigs, with a large circle of prominent Whig friends, including Fox and Sheridan. George enjoyed the friendship and hospitality of his relatives' Whig friends, and shared their initial enthusiasm for the French Revolution, but like many Whigs he was disillusioned by the Revolution's excesses. Moreover, his instincts were basically more conservative, much more in tune with the ideas of Burke than with those of Fox. He wrote at this time that although he was not so enthusiastically attached to the British consti-tution as to think it could not be improved, he did think it was the best practical constitution the world had ever seen. He never changed this opinion; he never supported parliamentary reform for fear it would upset the balance of the constitution.

Political apprenticeship

Altogether, Canning felt he could not commit himself to the Whigs. So in the summer of 1792 he got in touch with Pitt. He explained that as he could not afford to get himself into Parliament, he would be grateful if Pitt would find him a seat, in return for which he would give the Prime Minister his general support. Pitt presumably regarded him as a promising young recruit, and a year later a seat was found for him. Canning's political apprenticeship lasted from 1794, when he first entered Parliament, to Pitt's death almost exactly 12 years later.

The single most important thing about those 12 years politically was Canning's relationship with Pitt. Even when their friendship was severely strained by political disagreement it still dominated Canning's political life. Pitt for his part took a great deal of trouble encouraging and briefing Canning when he first went into the House of Commons. In January 1796 he made him one of two Under Secretaries at the Foreign Office under Lord Grenville. For someone who aspired to be 'a man of business' and not just a parliamentary debater, it was an excellent appointment. While Canning held this post, the government sent two peace missions to France under Lord Malmesbury. Neither was successful, but they provided Canning with a great deal of work and first-hand experience in the mysteries of diplomacy. For two summers running he was chained to his desk in Whitehall, dealing with incoming and outgoing dispatches while his friends escaped for long holidays in the country. He enjoyed himself, but there is no reason to suppose that at this early stage he had set his sights on becoming a great Foreign Secretary, and after two years' hard slog he may not have been sorry to be moved to a much less demanding post at the Board of Control, as the India Office was then called.

In February 1801, Canning's political world was thrown into complete disarray by Pitt's decision to resign because King George III refused to let him honour his implied promise to the Irish that Catholic emancipation – political equality – would be their reward if they agreed to the loss of their Parliament in Dublin. Canning insisted on resigning too, although as a junior member of the government, outside the Cabinet, he need not have done so, and Pitt tried hard to persuade him to stay on. Canning was also committed to Catholic emancipation but what seems to have moved him most strongly was his determination to sink or swim with Pitt. 'My story is a very short one,' he wrote, 'Pitt resigns, no matter for what reason, and I feel it right to follow him out of office.'[1]

Unfortunately he did not feel it right to follow Pitt's example and support the efforts of the new government, led by Henry Addington, to end the war with a compromise peace. Instead, he made it abundantly clear that he felt nothing but contempt for Addington and most of his team. After the Peace of Amiens had been signed in October 1801 he tried hard to persuade Pitt to turn Addington out. When in his own good time, after peace had broken down and the war was going badly, Pitt did turn Addington out, he did not explain why, and one can only speculate that after experiencing for four years how difficult and intolerant Canning could be, he had doubts about bringing him into his Cabinet team. Canning of course was bitterly disappointed, although the post he was given, Treasurership of the Navy, was a considerable promotion for him in the political hierarchy. Some 18 months later in December 1805, Pitt told Canning that he intended to bring him into the Cabinet in the New Year. But before he could carry out his intention, Pitt died.

Death of a patron

Although Canning was completely shattered by Pitt's death, from the point of view of his own career, as he himself realised, it was no bad thing that he should now have to emerge from Pitt's shadow. He was now 36 years old. Some six years earlier he had been lucky enough to fall in love with a girl who was also a considerable heiress. In fact her wealth at first deterred him from proposing to her because he did not want to be thought a fortune hunter. However, in the end they made a very happy marriage and Canning was able to dedicate himself to a political career without any serious financial worries. He never wanted to do anything else. He had no desire to set himself up as a country gentleman living on his estate, although when out of office he did go in for a little amateur farming, raising sheep to pass the time.

There was no obvious successor to Pitt as leader of the Tories, but there were several rising young politicians of roughly the same age and experience. Apart from Canning the most prominent were Castlereagh, Lord Hawkesbury, soon to have to move up to the House of Lords on the death of his father, Lord Liverpool, and Spencer Perceval, a distinguished lawyer. All three of these had had experience, if only briefly, of more senior posts than Canning had held. But a stronger bond was their devotion to Pitt's memory. They were known as Mr Pitt's Friends, and they were united in trying to preserve Pitt's measures and memory. But as one Whig politician, Samuel Romilly, commented, it surely was not very encouraging to a party to have no leader but one that is dead.[2]

Foreign Secretary 1807-9

They were not much better off with the man commissioned by the King to form a new government after he had quarrelled with, and dismissed, the Talents over the Catholic question. The Duke of Portland was not exactly at death's door – he died two years later – but he was an invalid, dependent on regular doses of laudanum and in no state to control his ministers or give them a proper lead. Only three members of his Cabinet sat in the Commons, Canning as Foreign Secretary, Castlereagh as Secretary for War and Colonies (the post he was holding when Pitt died), and Spencer Perceval as Chancellor of the Exchequer. Perceval, who was a pleasant, unpretentious man rather older than Canning and Castlereagh, was made Leader of the House of Commons, thus smothering for the time being the incipient rivalry between those two. By this time victory over the French was the overriding preoccupation of any government, and Canning would have preferred to go to the War Office rather than the Foreign Office. However, since Napoleon had by now, by force or by fear, extended his control over most of the continent, there was in fact rather more scope for diplomacy than for military operations.

Canning did everything he could through the diplomatic channels that were still open to impress on the Europeans that Britain was determined not to give up the struggle and they should not do so either. He had two ways of trying to influence events in Europe. The first was to try, in co-operation with Castlereagh, to prevent the small countries that still remained neutral, from knuckling under to Napoleon and tamely surrendering their assets, in particular their ships. In the case of the Danes, it was military and naval force, most especially the controversial bombardment of Copenhagen, more than diplomacy that extricated their fleet from Napoleon's clutches, and the operation had the unfortunate consequence of turning the furious Danes from neutrals into enemies. In the case of Portugal, Canning's forceful diplomacy succeeded in persuading the Portuguese ruler to flee to Brazil with the whole of the Portuguese fleet, only hours before the French marched into Lisbon. In that case diplomacy was again backed by force, in the shape of a squadron of the Royal Navy, but it did not have to be used.

Canning's second method of, as it were, inserting Britain into the conflict, was to let it be known through his diplomats that Britain would give generous financial help, and military too if possible, to any country that took up arms against Napoleon. This promise was fulfilled in 1808 when the Spaniards and the Portuguese rose against the French, and Sir Arthur Wellesley and Sir John Moore inaugurated the Peninsular campaigns.

The vice of over-ambition

We now come to a period of Canning's life when over some three years he made three disastrous mistakes and then had to live with the consequences for more than 10 years. His first mistake was to try to get

Castlereagh moved from the War Office. In the spring of 1809 the war in the Peninsula was indeed going badly, but Castlereagh, who was able, conscientious and very hardworking, did not deserve to be blamed for events beyond his control. Yet throughout the summer, Canning kept threatening to resign unless Castlereagh was moved to another post. When Castlereagh eventually learned what had been going on behind his back, he was naturally very angry. He challenged Canning to a duel which duly took place on Putney Heath, fortunately without serious consequence for either man. There was of course a lengthy post mortem about this dramatic encounter, in the press and in social and political circles. The strongest feelings seem to have been sympathy for Castlereagh and disapproval of Canning, whose behaviour appeared to be thoroughly underhand. (In fact he had wanted Castlereagh to be told what was going on but nobody had the nerve to do this.) Canning tried to justify himself in a published account of the affair but even his friends did not think much of it.

While all this was going on the Duke of Portland became seriously ill and had to resign. This prompted Canning to make his second major mistake: he resigned too, and made a barely concealed attempt to succeed Portland as Prime Minister. He refused to serve under Perceval, the most widely acceptable candidate, because of what he called 'the ordinary feelings of human nature', in other words, misplaced pride, and he told the King, in effect, that he was prepared to replace Perceval if he failed to form a government. The King was astonished: he called Canning's conversation the most extraordinary he had ever heard. Perceval accepted the post of Prime Minister with many misgivings but as the weeks and months passed he grew steadily in stature and in confidence.

Two and a half years after Canning had so blatantly overplayed his hand, the disastrous consequences were made clear. In May 1812, Spencer Perceval was shot through the heart by a madman in the lobby of the House of Commons, and if Canning had restrained his ambition and agreed to serve under Perceval he would have been in an excellent position to succeed him as Prime Minister. Instead, after some very complicated political manoeuvring, the prize fell to the worthy but uninspiring Lord Liverpool, and he kept it for the next 15 years. Canning refused to join his government on the grounds that it was known to be hostile to Catholic emancipation.

Later that summer, 1812, Canning made his third disastrous mistake. Lord Liverpool was anxious to strengthen his team in the House of Commons, where neither Castlereagh, the Foreign Secretary and Leader of the House, nor the other Cabinet ministers who sat there, were strong and effective speakers. So he removed what seemed to be the major stumbling block to bringing in Canning, by making his government neutral on the Catholic issue, and allowing individual ministers to take their own line on it. Then he engineered a meeting between Castlereagh and Canning at which the two rivals shook hands and agreed to let bygones be bygones.

Castlereagh even made the astonishingly magnanimous suggestion that Canning should go back to the Foreign Office. Canning later described this as perhaps the handsomest offer ever made to an individual but he turned it down, because Castlereagh refused to let him be Leader of the House of Commons as well. This meant, in Canning's view, that he would be serving, not with, but under Castlereagh, and he could only accept what he called perfect equality. The Prince Regent, the Prime Minister and friends tried to find a way round the difficulty but to no avail. So the upshot was that it was Castlereagh, not Canning, who in 1814–15, sat with the other representatives of the victorious powers in Vienna and Paris and rearranged the map of Europe.

Even this very brief summary of Canning's political vicissitudes between 1809 and 1812 shows clearly that he was far too ambitious for his own good. And I emphasise for his own good, since there is nothing wrong in being ambitious and Canning was without question extremely able. Moreover, he wanted office, not only for the honour and glory, certainly not for financial rewards, but because he really wanted, as he once said, to do some good. Afterwards, he said that at this period of his life he would have given 10 years of his life for two years in office. But his ambition clouded his political judgement and the result was a protracted and unnecessary setback to his career.

Canning and his colleagues

Canning was not a comfortable colleague because of his restless energy, his impatience, his occasionally sharp tongue, his general tendency to stir things up. On the other hand they knew he was a great asset. The very qualities that made him a difficult colleague around the Cabinet table, his brilliance and his domineering personality, made him invaluable in the House of Commons. He was a splendid speaker and debater, capable on occasion of electrifying and completely dominating the House. And at a time when party loyalties were very weak and many MPs prided themselves on their independence, it was very important to have a senior minister who could sway the House in important debates. It was a remarkable indication of Canning's reputation that when Lord Liverpool first became Prime Minister he felt that Canning was more of a threat than the Whig opposition.

Canning did have a personal following in the House of Commons of about a dozen – it had been more, but several of them lost their seats in the general election of 1812. This little group was unusually strictly disciplined and could make a significant difference in a close division.

But so far from making them the nucleus of a third party, he was so despondent about his political future that in the summer of 1813, he formally disbanded his little band of followers.

Return to office

Even without the Canningites, Liverpool would still have preferred to have Canning inside rather than outside the government, but it was not until early in 1816 that the Presidency of the Board of Control became vacant. The India Board was a very lowly Cabinet post, in the past not even included in the Cabinet. But Canning was a very chastened man, he accepted the post and settled down to work his way up the political ladder again.

Four years later, in the summer of 1820, further progress seemed permanently blocked, not because of any mistake or misjudgement of Canning's, but because George IV's estranged wife, Caroline of Brunswick, who had befriended Canning when he was a young politician, insisted on returning to England to claim her rights as Queen. After the proceedings against her in the House of Lords for alleged adultery had collapsed, Canning thought the Cabinet was proposing to deal too harshly with her and felt obliged to resign. Six months later, when Liverpool wanted to bring him back into the Cabinet, the King refused point blank. It was doubtful whether the King had a constitutional right to exclude a minister indefinitely for purely personal reasons, but Canning refused to let himself be made a bone of contention. He seems to have felt that his political career really was over, and it was only Castlereagh's suicide in August 1822 that stopped him from setting sail for Calcutta to become Governor General of India.

With great difficulty the King was persuaded to offer Canning the Foreign Secretaryship and also the post of Leader of the House of Commons. And having taught himself to look to India, Canning accepted this sudden turnaround, this fulfilment of his life's ambition, without enthusiasm:

> I would rather have been an absolute monarch [he meant in India], than a buffeted minister, but the fates have decreed otherwise, and the call of public duty, however unwelcome, must be obeyed.[3]

Foreign Secretary again

When Canning took over the Foreign Office in 1822, the change was more one of method and style than of substance. Castlereagh had worked closely with the rulers of Europe to hammer out the post-war agreements, and later, when he began to disagree with them, he still wanted to stay on friendly terms with them. Canning, on the other hand, had never met Metternich or the Tsar, and it did not bother him if they disliked or disapproved of him. He was more forthright, less diplomatic than Castlereagh had been. But in substance he continued the policy on which his predecessor had embarked when he found that the European autocracies, in particular Austria and Russia, were, to put it crudely, getting too big for their boots.

Castlereagh and Canning both believed that the powers should co-operate to preserve the territorial settlement of Europe, but when liberal revolts broke out, in Italy or in Spain, both Castlereagh and Canning strongly denied that the European powers had any right to intervene as policemen to restore the status quo.

Castlereagh had already begun to undermine the Congress system, when he refused to attend the Congress which met at Troppau in 1820 to deal with a revolt in Naples. Canning undermined it further the next year, when he instructed Wellington, the British representative at the Congress of Verona, to refuse, 'come what may', any British support, military or diplomatic, to the French if they invaded Spain to restore King Ferdinand, who had been toppled by a liberal revolt.[4]

Canning's aim, first, foremost and always, was to do whatever seemed necessary to maintain and increase Britain's prestige and prosperity. His second aim was to preserve European peace and stability by maintaining a balance between the European powers. He refused to intervene against liberal revolts not because he necessarily sympathised with them but because he could see no benefits to Britain, and perhaps considerable dangers, in helping autocratic rulers to interfere in the domestic affairs of other states. He tried, not always very successfully, to distinguish between national independence, of which he approved, and revolution, of which he did not. He only broke his rule of non-intervention once, when in 1824 he intervened diplomatically to install a pro-British government in Lisbon, because he felt that the alternative, a government subservient to the French, would be against British interests.

Canning began at the Foreign Office with a serious setback; in 1823–4 he failed to stop the French from invading Spain to restore King Ferdinand. He would not threaten war because he hated war, and Britain was under no treaty obligations to intervene militarily. He managed to persuade the House of Commons that he had done the best he could, and he was given a huge vote of confidence. But to be unable to stop the French from occupying Spain only a dozen years after Wellington had chased them out was a severe blow to Britain's prestige. It also aroused new fears of an over-mighty France. Moreover there were signs that the French intended to reconquer Spain's newly independent colonies in South America. Canning was determined to prevent this.

The South American question

His first idea to restrain the French was a public Anglo-American declaration that neither London nor Washington had any claim on the former Spanish colonies and would not allow them to be transferred to any other power. But this came to nothing because of the enormous American mistrust of the British and British intentions. President Monroe preferred to issue a unilateral declaration, the famous Monroe Doctrine. Canning was more successful with the French. He extracted from the French Ambassador, Prince de Polignac, a written undertaking known as the Polignac memorandum, that France would not try to intervene by force in South America. This undertaking was confirmed by the French government.

With the existence of the new American states established, Canning had to decide whether and when to accord them formal recognition. There were pressing commercial reasons for doing this without delay. British trade had suffered from the breakdown of law and order in the Caribbean, and British merchants were continually pressing the government to get the new South American governments to co-operate in protecting their commerce from the pirates. In October 1823 Canning sent consuls to Mexico, Colombia, Peru, Chile and Argentina. But he was reluctant to grant British recognition before Spain had done so because he felt that would be the most correct and legitimate procedure. He tried hard, but unsuccessfully, to persuade the King of Spain to acknowledge the independence of his former colonies. Before, however, going ahead with British recognition he felt he must be certain that the new states really were capable of leading an independent and stable existence, and since reliable information about most of them was sketchy, he sent Commissioners to two of the likeliest candidates, Colombia and Mexico. They both produced reports that he considered satisfactory.

The biggest obstacle to British recognition of any of the new South American states was the stubborn opposition of King George IV, and a conservative group of the Cabinet led by the Duke of Wellington. They only gave way when Canning and Liverpool both threatened to resign, and made it quite clear that they meant what they said.

At the time, Canning's recognition of the three South American countries at the end of 1824 and the beginning of 1825, was regarded as a great diplomatic triumph for Britain. It was also a blow to the whole Congress system, because for months during 1824 the other powers had discussed South America at a conference in Paris without any result. Canning had refused to attend unless the United States was also invited, to which the European monarchies would never agree. So he had been able to steal a march on them and make them look thoroughly ineffective. They were furious, but they could only protest.

For the South Americans, recognition by one of the major European powers was immensely important, and it made Britain easily the most influential European power in the region. So Canning's famous boast – 'I called the New World into existence to redress the balance of the Old' – although of course not literally true, was a dramatic way of summing up what the recognition had achieved for England. It became very famous, but far from being premeditated, it was part of an off-the-cuff response that Canning made in the House of Commons to an attack on his failure to prevent the French occupation of Spain. 'Our ancestors,' he said, 'had feared Spain because of her vast empire' so he had resolved that if France had Spain, it should be Spain without the Indies, by which he meant Spain without her colonies.[5]

Greece and Portugal

In the South American issue, Canning demonstrated the advantages of England acting alone. But he was a pragmatist, and he realised that in the case of the Greek revolt against the Turks, there was much to be said for joint action. Here the problem was not to crush the Greeks – on the contrary, Canning wanted to help them – but to prevent the Russians from going to their aid, and in the process overrunning the decrepit Ottoman Empire. In other words, it was to prevent Russian aggrandizement from upsetting the European balance of power. In this case Russia, not England, was the odd man out. Canning eventually decided that the best way to restrain the Russians would be by joining forces with them to try and impose mediation on the Turks, aiming to establish an autonomous Greece under Turkish suzerainty.

Wellington signed a protocol to this effect in St Petersburg in April 1826. In 1827, this was converted into a tripartite treaty, the Treaty of London, between Britain, France and Russia, which included a commitment to use force if necessary to end the fighting. This meant, in effect, stopping supplies and troops being sent from Egypt to Greece, and it was achieved in 1827 when the Allied fleets destroyed the Turkish navy in the bay of Navarino. The Greeks firmly believed that this spectacular victory, which Canning did not live to see, ensured their freedom.

The Treaty of London contained no binding guarantee of a future Greek state; Canning was in principle against committing Britain to any new territorial guarantees. But existing commitments were another matter; they had to be honoured. Britain was committed to defend Portugal, her oldest ally, against foreign aggression. In December 1826, a new constitutional Portuguese government invoked the treaty when Portuguese absolutists, backed by Spain, began to invade the country with the aim of restoring an absolutist regime. Canning responded at once. Troops were sent to Lisbon, and the mere fact of their arrival stopped the invasion. The crisis was part of the ideological struggle then being waged on the Continent, but Canning involved Britain solely on grounds of national honour. He told the Commons that they must fly to the aid of Portugal because it was their duty to do so.

> We go to plant the standard of England on the v. ... known heights of Lisbon. Where that standard is planted, foreign domination shall not come.[6]

The popular Foreign Secretary

Now that was the sort of language that the British public liked to hear. It made them feel good, and it made Canning extremely popular. He was the first Foreign Minister to realise that popular support at home would greatly strengthen his influence and authority abroad. He made public long extracts from his dispatches. He explained his policies in the House of Commons, and also to large public meetings; in those days, important speeches were reported at length and eagerly read in the press. This deliberate cultivation of popular support was greatly disliked by some of Canning's colleagues, especially by Wellington who thought it was degrading. To make matters worse, they did not much like the policies either. The King also, who already disliked Canning because of his friendship for Caroline, was outraged, and his outrage was stimulated by the foreign ambassadors and their wives, Russian, Austrian and French, who were already intriguing against Canning, and whom the King used to invite to private parties at Windsor. They were called 'the Cottage Coterie'. Eventually, however, the King realised that Canning was too popular to be got rid of, and that if he supported him he might acquire some of his popularity. Once Canning got the chance, it was not hard for someone of his charm and tact to win the King's personal regard as well as his support.

Premiership and the emancipation question

We now come to Canning's brief spell, barely four months, as Prime Minister. After Liverpool's stroke, on 18 February 1827, he was the obvious man to succeed him. He was the most senior minister in the Commons. He was extremely able and immensely popular. He was regarded by many people as indispensable. But he was, and always had been, a dedicated supporter of the Catholics' claim to political equality, and many Protestant politicians refused to serve under a pro-Catholic Prime Minister, even though the government remained neutral on the Catholic issue. The King too, felt he might be breaking his Coronation Oath if he accepted a pro-Catholic Premier. It is difficult today to understand the depth of hostility to Catholic emancipation, even among educated, level-headed men, far removed from 'No Popery' mobs. It arose out of their strong determination to safeguard the constitutional settlement of 1689 on which they believed the country's safety and stability depended. They feared that Catholic emancipation might dangerously undermine the Established Church which was an integral part of that settlement. Canning disagreed and he refused to be denied the Premiership simply because of his pro-Catholic views. In the end, after two months of doubt and discussion, the King asked Canning to form a government. Seven members of Liverpool's Cabinet, including Wellington and Peel, resigned at once, and so did about 40 others in lower posts. Canning had split the Tory Party, and when he turned to the Whigs to help make up his government, he split them too. Eventually after very protracted negotiations, three Whigs agreed to join the Cabinet, and several others accepted posts outside. For moderate Whigs, the chief obstacle to joining Canning was his opposition to parliamentary reform. But at that moment it was not being very much canvassed and in other respects Canning had much to recommend him: his liberal foreign policy, his support for Corn Law Reform, for Huskisson's economic reforms, for the abolition of slavery, above all, for his pro-Catholic views.

Ireland at that time was again seething with unrest, and the arrival of a champion of Catholic equality at 10 Downing Street might be expected to calm the situation, and give the Irish Catholics hope. Canning would certainly have wanted – would have felt he *ought* – to grant Catholic emancipation. Whether he could have overcome the opposition of the ultra-Protestants in Parliament as successfully as Wellington and Peel did two years later, is another matter. With Ireland apparently on the verge of revolt after O'Connell's election victory in County Clare, they were able to argue that there was no alternative to emancipation, without acknowledging, as Canning had always done, that political equality for Catholics was in itself both right and just.

Notes

(1) Bagot, J. F. *George Canning and His Friends* Vol. 1 (John Murray, 1909) p. 180.
(2) Quoted in Gray, Denis *Spencer Perceval* (Manchester University Press, 1963). p. 59.
(3) Harewood MSS, 10. (14 September 1822).
(4) Wellington Despatches, N. S., vol. 1, p. 304.
(5) Parl. Deb. N. S. XVI, 309/97 (12 December 1826).
(6) Parl. Deb. N. S. XVI, 350/69 (12 December 1826).

Wendy Hinde is the biographer of George Canning and is currently working on the Catholic emancipation question.

J. R. Dinwiddy
English Radicalism before the Chartists

The late J. R. Dinwiddy analyses the background to and nature of the radicalism in the decade of Peterloo.

The term 'radical' came into use in English as a political label in the years around 1820. Though it was subsequently used much more broadly, to describe any kind of reformer, it originally had a fairly specific meaning. It meant a supporter of the programme of radical parliamentary reform which was the object of a large-scale agitation around the time of Peterloo. The central item in this programme was manhood suffrage (often loosely described at the time as 'universal' suffrage), though it also included annual elections and secret voting; and *radical* reformers were frequently contrasted with *moderate* reformers, who preferred less sweeping measures such as household suffrage and triennial parliaments. The radical programme was not new. It had been advocated in the 1770s by Major John Cartwright (who was still active as a reform campaigner in the 1820s), and it had been adopted in the early 1790s by the first associations of working-class reformers, such as the London Corresponding Society.

Radicalism during the revolutionary wars

In the 1790s, something of a political polarisation had taken place. On the one hand the plebeian societies, for whose members the French Revolution had opened up new possibilities of change, committed themselves enthusiastically to thoroughgoing democracy; on the other hand the bulk of the propertied classes, influenced by Burke and the disorders in France, became increasingly conservative and 'anti-Jacobin'. Moderate reform, meanwhile, was out of fashion. It was advocated by the Association of the Friends of the People, which was formed by several liberal-minded members of the aristocracy and gentry in 1792, but this body received very little support in the country at large. Radical reform attracted much more numerous support; though it was not yet an issue that aroused general interest among working people, there were a few places such as Sheffield and Norwich where the bulk of the artisan population seemed to be in favour of it.

However, in the later 1790s – owing partly to the wartime pressure for loyalty and solidarity, partly to widespread disenchantment with the kind of political experimentation that had been tried in France, and partly to repressive legislation affecting public meetings and the press – the whole question of reform became difficult if not impossible to keep alive. This remained true for more than a decade, and interest in the question did not revive on a significant scale until 1809–10. In these years, much indignation was aroused by revelations of corrupt practices in the public service (such as the sale of army commissions by a mistress of the Commander-in-Chief), and by failures in the management of the war (such as the disastrous expedition to the island of Walcheren off the Dutch coast); and when Parliament declined to take action against those widely perceived as responsible, the idea spread that Parliament itself should be made to represent the views and interests of the public more satisfactorily. William Cobbett's writings in his *Political Register* were particularly vivid and persistent in exposing the corruptions of what he called 'the system'; Cartwright was equally persistent (though much less vivid) in linking these to the paramount need for parliamentary reform; and Sir Francis Burdett, the aristocratic tribune of the people who had been elected MP for Westminster in opposition to both the established parties in 1807, spoke out boldly for the redress of popular grievances.

At this stage, when the reform question was being brought back to the surface of politics after some years of submersion, there was no mention of universal suffrage, partly because it was feared that such a demand would reactivate conservative alarmism. The programme which Burdett outlined in the House of Commons in July 1809, after consultation with Cartwright, Cobbett and others, did not go beyond the enfranchisement of those who paid direct taxes; and indeed support for the reform agitation was coming mainly (as the *Morning Chronicle* commented on 17 April 1809) from 'the yeomanry, the housekeepers [i.e. householders] and the middle ranks of society' – those sections of the community which were suffering most immediately from fiscal burdens such as the income tax.

A year or two later, in 1811–12, there was a great deal of hardship and discontent among working people in the industrial areas, owing to a combination of harvest failure and wartime dislocations of trade. There were food riots in many parts of the country, and in the northern counties and the East Midlands the Luddites broke machinery in attempts to extract concessions from employers. There was also, as there had been in the years of repression around the turn of the century, a certain amount of plotting by would-be revolutionaries. But this did not develop into a serious threat, and popular protest at this time did not in general take a political form.

The post-war revival of radicalism

In the post-war period, however, a variety of factors helped to produce a revival, and indeed a massive extension, of the popular radicalism which had first emerged in the early 1790s. One broad factor which lay behind this development was the failure of alternative means of redressing working-class grievances. Luddism, dramatic and menacing though it was for a few months, was suppressed by the summer of 1812. As for more peaceful methods, pressure from trade unions was of limited effectiveness, partly because the Combination Acts of 1799 and 1800 had made them illegal, and partly because population growth had produced a relative abundance of labour which strengthened the bargaining position of employers. Efforts were made to secure the enforcement or extension of earlier legislation which had provided some protection for the interests of certain categories of working men. But the current of opinion – among the propertied classes at least – was running strongly in favour of *laissez-faire* (except where the interests of those classes seemed to require forms of state intervention such as protection for agriculture or the banning of workmen's combinations). During the war, Parliament responded negatively to proposals for the fixing of minimum wages for agricultural labourers and hardloom weavers. Moreover, the apprenticeship clauses of the Elizabethan Statute of Artificers, by which entry to certain crafts had been restricted to those who had served seven-year apprenticeships, were actually repealed in 1814, despite numerous petitions from journeymen for their retention; and Parliament was seen to be sanctioning and facilitating the displacement of skilled by semi-skilled labour in the trades concerned.

Besides this mounting evidence of Parliament's unresponsiveness to working-class demands, a direct cause of the spread of radical ideas in the postwar period was the economic depression which struck in 1816–17 and again in 1819. This gave particular urgency to feelings of discontent, especially when people were expecting the return of peace to bring better conditions. Also, distress could be seen as to some extent political in origin, because the burden of taxation continued to be heavy. Though the income tax was repealed in 1816, a large revenue was still needed (principally to pay the interest on the national debt, which had more than tripled during the war). There was an increasing realisation that the mass of the population was providing most of the revenue through the payment of *indirect* taxes on consumer goods; and the clear implication was that if there was to be 'no taxation without representation' those subject to direct taxation were not the only people who ought to be enfranchised.

Radical organisations and newspapers

In 1817 Cartwright, responding to a grassroots demand from the newly formed 'Hampden Clubs' of industrial England, reverted to the policy of manhood suffrage which he had advocated in the late eighteenth century, and Cobbett (who was shifting the focus of his journalism to a working-class audience) embraced this measure for the first time. But the person who was the most conspicuous spokesman of working-class radicalism in the postwar years was Henry 'Orator' Hunt. He did not come from the industrial working classes himself, any more than Cartwright or Cobbett did, and he does not appear to have had much detailed understanding of the situation and needs of the various occupational groups which made up this section of the population. Yet from 1816 until the early 1830s he was particularly staunch in devoting his own political life to the promotion of a democratic programme of reform, and he earned himself a loyal following in the North and Midlands by consistently calling for manhood suffrage on the grounds that labour as well as property deserved the recognition and protection afforded by the franchise.

In the years between Waterloo and Peterloo – as was the case later, in the 1840s – radical agitation took three main forms, which to a large extent reinforced each other. One was a campaign conducted through the press. Cobbett led the way, from November 1816, in producing cheap political commentaries (his weekly 'twopenny trash' as the Conservative press characterised it) for a mass readership, but he fled to America in March 1817 to avoid arrest when the Habeas Corpus Act was suspended. Thereafter, though Cobbett's *Register* continued to appear, T. J. Wooler's *Black Dwarf* became the most prominent of the radical periodicals, lasting from 1817 to 1824. Others, while sometimes more militant in tone than the publications of Cobbett and Wooler, were more ephemeral (with the notable exception of Carlyle's *Republican*, 1819–26). But a radical press with a wide circulation did establish itself in the post-war period, and did much to give coherence and unity of purpose to the popular reform movement.

The second element in the agitation which helped to give it coherence (at least at certain times) was the formation of radical associations. The initial wave of these, which owed much to the proselytising efforts of Major Cartwright, consisted of several dozen Hampden Clubs and Union Societies formed in the winter of 1816–17. They were most numerous among the handloom weavers of South Lancashire and the stocking-weavers of the East Midlands, though there were others in South Yorkshire and at places such as Birmingham and Norwich. Some of the clubs sent out delegates or 'missionaries' to communicate with other parts of the country. They also organised petitions to Parliament, and in January 1817, a meeting of some 60 deputies from petitioning bodies was held in London to agree on a plan of reform. (It was on this occasion that the movement's preference for universal over household suffrage was made decisively apparent.) Under the impact of the repressive legislation passed in the spring of 1817, the Hampden Clubs withered, but a further batch of organisations came into being in 1818–19. The initiatives came originally from Hull, where a society of Political Protestants was formed ('for the purpose of protesting against the mockery of our indisputable right to a real representative') in July 1818. The society was given publicity by the *Black Dwarf*, and during the next year or so many similarly constituted societies were formed elsewhere, notably in the North East, which had previously been little involved in radical agitation.

The third important element in the campaign for radical reform was the staging of public meetings. Precedents had been set in the mid-1790s by the London Corresponding Society, but the 'platform' strategy was particularly associated with 'Orator' Hunt (and later with the Chartist, Feargus O'Connor, whose political style was consciously modelled on Hunt's). The essence of the strategy was to use the constitutional right of public assembly, and a militant brand of rhetoric which stopped only just short of incitement to violence, in order to mobilise people in vast numbers, to inspire them with a sense of collective strength, and to convince parliament and the ruling classes that the popular demand for reform was irresistible. Notable examples of the use of this strategy were the mass meetings held in the winter of 1816–17 in Spa Fields, London (at which Hunt was the main speaker) and on Newhall Hill outside Birmingham, and the four great regional demonstrations held in the summer of 1819 at Birmingham, Leeds, London and Manchester. The last of these, of course, was the occasion of the 'Peterloo massacre'. The meeting in St Peter's Fields, to which contingents of people marched in with drums and banners from the towns and villages around Manchester, was intended to be intimidating, even though arms were not being carried by the demonstrators. The authorities were almost being *challenged* to take some action against the crowd, and thereby to outrage public opinion; and indeed the sending in of the yeomanry did present the radicals with a great moral advantage in the aftermath of the meeting.

The weaknesses of the radicals

In the last resort, however, the regime proved strong enough not only to survive but to do so without making concessions. Though the opposition in Parliament was keen to make capital out of the 'massacre' for the purpose of discrediting the government, the propertied classes were almost solidly hostile to the democratic programme which Hunt and his followers were pursuing. Also, the government had the backing of a standing army in which discipline was maintained by an appallingly brutal system of corporal punishment; the radicals, on the other hand, had little or no access to weapons beyond rough pikes manufactured by local blacksmiths. A further fact of great importance was that there were only a few parts of the country – most of them remote from the centre of power in London – where the working classes were sufficiently concentrated and politicised to mount any serious collective action. There was mass support for radicalism in the Manchester area, in the West Riding of Yorkshire, in the East Midlands; but the postwar agitation was far less of a *national* movement than Chartism was to be.

There were a few episodes in the years we have been considering when agitation went underground and preparations were made for the use of *physical* force. The occasions when its use was actually attempted were hardly impressive. On 2 December 1816, when a large crowd had gathered in Spa Fields, Islington, to hear Hunt speak at a reform meeting, a group of ultra-radicals led a few hundred men off into the City, where they sacked some gunshops with the intention of mounting an armed attack on the Tower of London; but no attack was attempted, and the city magistrates were soon able to restore order. On the night of 8 June 1817 two or three hundred men from the villages to the south of Huddersfield assembled to make an assault on the town, but dispersed when they were met by a patrol of yeomanry; and on the following night, in the so-called Pentrich Rising, a group of similar size which was marching on Nottingham behaved in a similar way when it was confronted by a score of troops.

In February 1820, a meeting of conspirators was raided in a loft in Cato Street, off the Edgware Road in London, when it was planning (as the authorities knew through a spy within the group) to assassinate the cabinet at one of its weekly dinners. A few weeks later, on the night of 11–12 April, a band of insurgents marched from Barnsley to Grange Moor outside Huddersfield, but broke up when the other contingents they were expecting to meet there failed to materialise. In both 1817 and 1820, the amount of insurrectionary conspiracy was certainly greater than the very small scale of these incidents would suggest. In 1817, it is true, such plotting may have been encouraged by a government agent, 'Oliver the Spy'; but it appears that in the early months of 1820, after the Six Acts had outlawed public or 'constitutional' agitation, an autonomous and fairly widespread plan for a 'general rising' existed among working men in parts of the northern counties and South West Scotland. In both years, however, the problems involved in secretly concerting the activities of scattered groups of revolutionaries, in the face of a loose but not ineffective system of surveillance operated by the Home Office and magistrates, were very apparent. It should be emphasised that although there *was* a revolutionary strand in working-class politics during the second decade of the century, it was a minor strand compared to the 'constitutional' one, and the outstanding radical leaders of the time steered clear of it.

Radicals and the Reform Bill

The post-war reform movement was undoubtedly the principal phase of early nineteenth-century radicalism, and as we have seen, it foreshadowed Chartism in most of its central features. For some time after 1820, the country enjoyed relative prosperity and low food prices, and much of the effort which had gone into radical politics was diverted into other channels such as trade unionism and the co-operative movement. When the demand for political reform revived around 1830, the campaign which developed was a very different one from that which had led up to Peterloo. By this stage, middle-class elements in the new towns were gaining in confidence and were coming to regard a heavily aristocratic and Anglican regime as inadequate to the country's needs; and the Whig Party, after decades of hesitancy, was ready to tie its fortunes to the cause of parliamentary reform. The Whig Reform Bill – more far-reaching than most contemporaries had expected, yet preserving what was seen as defensible in the old system – won overwhelming support for the middle classes and at least partial acceptance within the landowning élite. At the same time, the measure sharply divided the radicals. By some, it was welcomed as a substantial first instalment. To others it seemed no better than a sham: it extended the circle of power to embrace most people of property, but it offered no participation or security to working men. It was Hunt above all who voiced the latter point of view, and he was backed by 'Unions of the Working Classes' in London and the North which denounced the Bill and called for a genuinely democratic reform. It was only after the Bill had been passed, however, that his interpretation of it came to be generally adopted in working-class circles. As is well known, disillusionment over the Reform Act, plus indignation over the New Poor Law and a general resentment at the reformed parliament's lack of concern for the unenfranchised, were important causes of the next and greatest phase in the history of popular radicalism.

Further Reading

Belchem, J. *'Orator' Hunt: Henry Hunt and English Working Class Radicalism* (Oxford University Press, 1985).
Calhoun, C. *The Question of Class Struggle: Social Foundations of Popular Radicalism during the Industrial Revolution* (Basil Blackwell, 1982).
Dinwiddy, J. R. *From Luddism to the First Reform Bill* (Basil Blackwell, 1986).

Epstein, J. 'Understanding the cap of liberty: symbolic practice and social conflict in early nineteenth-century England', *Past and Present*, No. 122, 75–118 (1989).

McCalman, I. *Radical Underworld: Prophets, Revolutionaries, and Pornographers in London* (Cambridge University Press, 1988).

Read, D. *Peterloo: The 'Massacre' and its Background* (Manchester University Press, 1958).

Royle, E. and Walvin, J. *English Radicals and Reformers 1760–1848* (Harvester Press, 1982).

Rule, J. *The Labouring Classes in Early Industrial England 1750–1850* (Longman, 1988).

Thomis, M. and Holt, P. *Threats of Revolution in Britain 1789–1848* (Macmillan, 1977).

Thompson, E. P. *The Making of the English Working Class*, 2nd edn. (Penguin, 1968).

The late J. R. Dinwiddy was Professor of Modern History at Royal Holloway and Bedford New College, London.

PART II
Reform

The first two years of the 1830s were dominated by the struggle which culminated in the passage of the Whigs' Reform Act. The electoral qualifications in English boroughs varied enormously; so the Reform Act instituted a single £10 householder franchise. This was accompanied by a degree of redistribution; boroughs with less than 2,000 inhabitants (not electors) lost both seats and those with 2–4,000 lost one. Twenty-two new boroughs were created; many were centres of new manufacturing. All boroughs with over 4,000 inhabitants had two MPs. They were to represent interests, not head of population. The result was that the borough franchise continued to be dominated by small market towns.

The counties, with their larger and more popular electorate of 40 shilling freeholders, had been the more satisfactory element in the electoral system. The only changes here, therefore, were the addition of electors of equivalent status — the leaseholders, copyholders and £50 tenants-at-will. In addition, 65 seats were gained from the boroughs, which nevertheless remained over-represented.

The effect of the separate legislation for Ireland was more limited. The raising of the Irish county franchise to £10 in 1829 was retained and Ireland was given five more MPs. The Scottish legislation had a more substantial effect; the electorate rose from 5,000 to 65,000 and the seats were redistributed.

Despite these reforms patrons were still able to control some 50 borough seats. Many seats continued to be uncontested. Where contests did take place they were often as colourful, and even more expensive for the candidates, than before 1832. The composition of Parliament stayed much the same. Radicals were disappointed both with the Act and other Whig measures such as the New Poor Law.

However, the balance of the old Constitution had been destroyed. The power of the king to choose his ministers was replaced by the power of the increased electorate to choose them for him. Political attention meanwhile shifted to the development of party organisation to win the favours of this electorate. In 1841 an electoral verdict was, for the first time, to bring about a change of government. The Tories, who had been decimated in the election following the Reform Act, were ironically returned to power.

Norman McCord
The Age of Reform

The reform legislation of the 1830s and 1840s has been criticised for its limitations. Norman McCord examines the background to reform and the difficulties which legislators and the new administrators faced in making the changes which did take place.

The period between 1815 and 1870 saw changes of cardinal importance. In these years Britain developed into the world's first great industrial society. It also offers to the student one of history's most fascinating stories, the spectacle of the transition of British government and society from what is at the beginning of this period essentially a decentralised rural society.

Although in 1815 Britain had increasingly important urban centres and a nascent industrial base it was still overwhelmingly a rural society. It was not until the 1851 census that the majority of the population was shown as living in towns. Towns for the purposes of the 1851 census, it should also be remembered, included small market towns such as Alnwick, Hexham and Wooler, which remained intimately associated with the surrounding countryside, as well as new urban centres of industry such as Manchester, Bolton and Bradford. There was therefore a substantial countryside element in the narrow urban majority registered in 1851.

Not only was Britain in 1815 a decentralised rural society facing unprecedented and unforeseeable economic pressures, social change and accelerating population growth, but it faced these difficulties with a notable record of relatively little internal conflict and bloodshed as compared with virtually all contemporary societies.

These decades were also of importance in the development of British government and administration and the resulting transformation of Britain, from the early nineteenth century, from a little-governed nation to a nation in which the machinery of national and local government was expected to carry out many more functions than had ever previously been required of it.

The enormous condescension of posterity

Perhaps one of the problems in some interpretations of this period is that there has been a temptation to look at the age of reform in too judgemental a manner. We tend for instance, to criticise early

Victorian society for failing to match standards of altruism and virtue which have proved beyond any human society. Indignation is often the response felt to some of the historical evidence we have about the experience of British society in this period. This may illustrate a worthy idealism, but it does not necessarily advance understanding amongst students of history. The absence of trade unions from prehistoric society and the failure of Elizabethan England to create a National Health Service are, I suppose, regrettable if understandable. It is, however, astonishing how much twentieth-century writing on nineteenth-century history has greatly resembled in tone the absurdity of such notions. At whatever level we are studying history we have to try to remember that the proper task of the student of history is to try to explain what did happen and if you find yourselves arguing that something else should have happened instead you are merely advertising the fact that you have failed to understand the historical process and context. We have to avoid, to borrow E. P. Thompson's splendid phrase, 'the enormous condescension of posterity'. Edward Thompson applied that phrase to the radical movements of the early nineteenth century, but it can be applied much more widely, not least to those whose responsibility it was to guide the society of the time through particularly difficult years.

My focus in this article will be the work of governments during the age of reform, and especially to discuss the ways the governments of the 1830s and 1840s tried to use legislation, the civil service and agencies of reform. If these matters are to be appreciated they have to be seen firmly in the light of the realities of the society in which these governments and would-be reformers operated and the resources which that society actually possessed. It is easy for us, with the benefit of hindsight, to see that the expansion of government in this period was to become a major method of tackling many social problems. It is equally clear that this was a lesson which was learnt very slowly and reluctantly by nineteenth-century administrators and politicians. Our task is to explain why this is what happened, rather than resorting to arbitrary criticisms.

Before legislation could be used for social reform at least two major ingredients were necessary. One was the resources in men and administrative capacity, and the other was the will to create those resources. Looking at the circumstances of this period gives us a greater sense of the administrative possibilities of the time.

The social context of reform

The 1831 census credited Great Britain with a population of only 16.5m. It was still largely a rural society and still largely dependent upon agriculture. For the most part people lived in much smaller communities than we do now and for most people life was much more bounded by local considerations. These local circumstances existed in extremely varied forms, and this in itself posed difficulties in devising and applying national reforms. For example, the 1834 Poor Law Amendment Act was intended to cover the whole of England and Wales. However, the effect of what was intended to be a piece of standardising legislation was very different depending on the local conditions in which it was applied. So, for example, if one looks at the Hendon Poor Law Union, a wealthy, sophisticated area quite near London, the 1834 legislation swiftly produced an active local authority willing to take action in such areas as public health, education, and provision of specialist facilities for such groups as the mentally ill amongst the poor. Now if instead of looking at authorities in the Home Counties we consider one in rural North Wales we receive an entirely different picture. Poor Law Unions in North Wales tended to be very large and, because of the low rateable value of local property, very short of funds. Of one of them it was said that even those who paid poor rates seldom ate meat and some of the guardians were removed on the grounds of pauperism. And yet the government was trying to devise a national policy which would meet such varying local conditions.

It is perhaps not easy, in an age of speedy communications and mass media, to appreciate readily the strength and importance of local circumstances, nor the social cohesion of these small rural communities which later developments in British society have tended to erode. Britain in this period was not an equal or democratic society. Great inequalities of status, influence and opportunity were the norm. However, we should always be careful to remember that there was nothing new about this. There was no 'Merrie England' of equality in the past, despite the historical myths on which radical reformers of the nineteenth century fed. Even the modest extent of democracy and equality attained in the twentieth century lay well in the future and was scarcely even a widespread dream in the early years of the nineteenth century.

Limited government resources

In terms of the formal agencies of government, Britain in 1815 possessed only very limited resources. When Sir Robert Peel became Home Secretary in 1822 the Home Office, the most important domestic department of state, possessed a headquarters staff of about 20. The headquarters staff of the Board of Trade in 1840 numbered about 30. The arrangements for the recruitment of these tiny groups of civil servants were not very efficient. Patronage remained, as it always had been, the basis for appointment, and arrangements for retirement and pensions were not well organised. Let me give one example from the Admiralty. The Admiralty was not only a key mainstay of defence in an uncertain world, but was also one of the biggest spenders among government departments. The cardinal position of secretary of this department was held, with one brief interval, by Sir John Barrow from 1804 until he was, with considerable difficulty, persuaded to retire at the age of 80 in 1845.

We must therefore put out of our minds any idea that the governments of this period had anything approaching unlimited powers and capacity, or sophisticated administrative machinery. When the Whigs took office in 1830 there had been only three national censuses and all of those had been limited and imperfect in the information that they had gathered. At this time there were not even reliable maps of Britain in any systematic form, although the Ordnance Survey was to remedy this in the ensuing decades. Arrangements for drafting Acts of Parliament were extremely haphazard and unplanned. So in a whole variety of ways the administration machine was very limited, greatly limiting the scope and efficiency of government in these years.

The importance of land and position

But it was less damaging than it appears at first sight, for in the early nineteenth century the cohesion of British society did not depend on the formal agencies of government. Throughout the age of reform, and especially in its early years, British society was much more held together and controlled by a great mass of unofficial disciplines, controls and power. These included the power relating to inherited wealth and position. Possessions and education were more important in controlling society than formal office in local and central government.

These two areas of power are not of course separate. The ruling minorities who controlled the economic and social aspects of British society also dominated both local and central government. The nature of this connection is well illustrated in the key officers in local government. In the 1830s and 1840s you did not become important by being appointed a county magistrate, you would only be appointed a county magistrate because you were already important.

The desire for cheap, efficient government

In this traditional, property-governed, society, the dominant minorities, and not only the dominant minorities, were deeply suspicious of attempts to extend the scope of government and the number of government agencies. Not the least of the reasons behind this attitude was the awareness that government is paid for by the confiscation of resources from other members of society in the form of taxes.

37

Not only was this a society in which government was controlled by these groups of rate-payers and tax-payers who also financed its activities, it was a society in which government did not have a particularly good reputation. It was well known that from time immemorial governments had used their powers of patronage for partisan political purposes. There had been some movement away from the worst abuses since the economical reforms of the 1780s, but the process was far from complete. If we consider some of the appointments made by the reforming Whigs to the new civil service posts that they created it is clear that partisan patronage was not dead. For example, James Stuart of the factory inspectors, Sir John Walsham of the Assistant Poor Law Commissioners and H. S. Tremenheere, who held a variety of government appointments, were all very closely connected to the party which appointed them. Tremenheere owed his first government appointment to the fact, according to one contemporary, that he was 'the only Whig in the family'. Nor was patronage something that only corrupt politicians resorted to. Anyone who was in public office in these years was subject to intense pressure to use his influence to provide jobs for supporters. Government patronage in constituencies tended to be channelled through friendly MPs. There was no fairness in the distribution of official patronage.

Associated with all this is the fact that one of the most powerful political cries in the nineteenth century is the demand for cheap government and low taxation. Throughout the nineteenth century it can usually be said that demand for cheap government was more popular than any countervailing cry for bigger and better administration. It existed in all reaches of British society. Even in radical propaganda of the period, accusations of government waste, government extravagance, government inefficiency and possible government corruption appeared much more frequently than any constructive proposals for arming the government, through higher taxation, with new resources to tackle the major social problems facing that society. Certainly in the Britain of the 1830s and 1840s it is not possible to see any widespread or continuous pressure for increased government expenditure. Where expansion took place and expenditure did increase it was usually because of the activities of small ranks of dedicated reformers, who were usually members of the dominant élite, and, not infrequently within government itself, working with the increasingly clear facts about the nature of problems that were becoming available. However the demand for cheap government remained a major limitation on reform in the 1830s and 1840s and for many years afterwards.

The effect of this was marked on the Whigs in the 1830s. The principal Whig slogan of these years was what was described as Lord Grey's motto, 'Peace, Retrenchment and Reform'. For many of his followers peace meant cutting the costs of the armed forces, retrenchment meant cutting government spending and reform meant the removal of those indefensible elements in the constitution which had facilitated the corruption and extravagance of government. In the early 1830s, the Whigs cut taxation by 10%. For many of their supporters this was a more important and valuable achievement than the reforms for which they have subsequently been better known.

Parliamentary reform

Detailed examination of some of the reforms of the 1830s allows amplification of these points. It must be clear that the Great Reform Act was not based upon any searching or accurate knowledge or assessment of the nature of contemporary society. A major point in the arguments of the reformers was their acceptance of a broad, but extremely vague, notion of a middle class, endued with certain virtues. Close scrutiny reveals that it is actually very difficult to find the middle class that the Whigs talked about so much in the 1830s. It is likely that the tenant farmers came as near as any group in the period to being a coherent and articulate middle class. They were part of the dominant agricultural interest and extremely varied.

The principal support for parliamentary reform in the early 1830s came from within the governing minorities in that highly unequal society. The kind of reform that the Whigs were proposing in 1831 evoked widespread support amongst powerful and influential interests. The 'country' interest had long regarded the pocket and rotten boroughs as a basis for government corruption and the Whig bill seemed to meet these objections. The proposers were people like Durham and Grey, who were themselves leading aristocratic landowners. Furthermore, the bill would entail a reduction in the number of borough seats and a considerable extension of county representation.

The Tories knew that by opposing the bill they had alienated much of their support. The Whigs knew that they could count on not merely the noisy and embarrassing support of radicals but also on the bulk of 'respectable' opinion. The 1831 general provided the Whigs with a decisive majority for reform, on the old unreformed franchise and on the old unreformed distribution of seats. In some places enthusiasm and agitation for reform played some part, but the overwhelming swing of the county seats to reform in 1831 is not to be explained by mass working-class movements. In Northumberland for instance, a county dominated by landowners with strong Tory traditions, it swiftly became clear to the popular sitting Tory member Matthew Bell, in the course of a canvass he conducted against the Reform Bill, that even Northumberland could not be held against it.

The wide support for reform in 1831 enabled the Whigs to pass the measure. The reason for their decline in the later 1830s was because they could not hold, on other issues, the amount of establishment support they had gathered in 1831–32. If this support had been united against reform in 1832 it is difficult to see how any practicable bill could have been before parliament at all.

The problem of franchise qualifications

Many of the problems the Whigs encountered in enacting the Reform Bill are of interest in illustrating the problems of government in these years. They were not trying to enact democratic reform, and there is no reason why they should have done. What they were trying to do was remove the more indefensible aspects of the system and recruit to the political nation groups who could be seen as useful. They sought to admit the responsible, respectable, trustworthy few and to exclude the dangerous many. But how? The Whigs could not use an age test for eligibility to the franchise as we do now, because there was no registration of births. This is why the 1832 Reform Act instead relied on property qualifications, the evidence for which was already in existence. In the counties the freehold, leasehold and the tenancy qualifications could all be proved by existing documentation in the form of tax or rent receipts. In the boroughs the famous ten pound housing qualification was not new. What was done in 1832 was to take a qualification which was already being used in another area of government action and apply it to the franchise. Such qualifications had been used in the assessments for the house tax for many years and as recently as 1825 the exemption limit for the house tax was ten pounds. The use of this qualification was a practical solution to a most difficult problem.

The Whigs often talked in 1831–32 of trying to enfranchise the property and intelligence of the nation. It might seem that these two qualities do not naturally go together. However it is important to remember at this juncture that intelligence had a different meaning in the early nineteenth century. What the Whigs intended was the enfranchisement of the possessors of property and information. By this they meant those who could make an informed use of the vote. In a world in which education was predominantly the prerogative of property the equation of property and intelligence was not stupid. And these men were far from stupid.

It is interesting to see how some of the new constituencies of 1832 chose to use the new powers they were given. The enfranchisement of the newly industrialised boroughs is one of the most remarkable features of the 1832 Act. It is odd what some of these new boroughs chose to do with their suffrages. Milner Gibson, a landowner and ex-Tory, was MP for Manchester from 1841 to 1857. But the most remarkable was the borough of Wolverhampton, which still holds the record for an MP's uninterrupted tenure of a seat. From 1835 to 1898, one of the Wolverhampton MPs was the Hon. Charles Pelham Villiers, the son of the Earl of Clarendon. The extent to which industrial Britain was truly radical can easily be exaggerated.

The New Poor Law

Let us consider another major reform of these years, the Poor Law Amendment Act of 1834. What the government could do in this matter was limited by what ratepayers and taxpayers could stand and by the continuing strong sense of local community in that society. There was a strong belief that the local community should be responsible for its own poor. The New Poor Law of 1834 was therefore a mixture of the old and new. The New Poor Law unions were not created by the drawing of rational boundaries on maps, but by the grouping together of existing parishes. Those parishes continued to play an important part in poor relief for many years after 1834. Firstly, it is the parishes which elected the poor law guardians.

More importantly, each parish remained responsible for paying the cost of its own poor. It was not until the Union Chargeability Act of 1865 that within a poor law union the rate was levied uniformly. The continuing responsibility of parishes until then placed a crippling strain on the new system. In Newcastle upon Tyne, for instance, if you lived in any of the increasingly suburban parishes such as Jesmond, you did not have to pay a penny to the maintenance of the poor of All Saints parish down by the quayside, which was, as the rich moved outwards, increasingly a festering mass of poverty, disease and degradation. In South Shields, if you were a shipowner who lived in Westoe you did not have to pay a penny to the old quayside parishes with their poverty, unemployment, sickness and slums.

Implementing reform

Equally important, when the Whigs created new governmental machinery in the 1830s this often required the services of increasing numbers of officials. Where were these to come from? In the case of the new poor law there was only one obvious reservoir of potential officials, and that was in the officials of the old poor law. They turned out to be a very mixed bag indeed. Similar problems attended the creation of the Metropolitan Police in 1829 and the provincial police forces throughout the nineteenth century. There was no large reservoir of potential trained officials waiting to be utilised. However, within this inherently unequal society there were men from within the governing élites, who were willing to take on new administrative responsibilities within expanded government activity.

This was of extreme importance in the world of the 1830s and 1840s. If, to implement the New Poor Law, the central government had sent in civil servants, they would have found it extremely difficult to make progress in the face of local vested interests. Instead they were able to call upon a small group of men of independent status and influence who were able to take on the new roles of inspectors of factories, of railways, of schools, of mines and assistant poor law inspectors. These men brought to the new posts an inherent authority of their own, as a result of their social position. A very good example is Sir John Walsham, Bt., who was the man responsible for the introduction of the New Poor Law in North East England. He was a landowner on the Welsh borders and deputy lord lieutenant of Herefordshire and Radnorshire, and connected with leading members of the Whig government. In his governmental post he could talk to magnates on their own terms, whilst most of the guardians treated him with deference. He was, incidentally, brother-in-law of the well-connected local Tory MP, Matthew Bell, who was not only a local landowner, coal-owner, bank and railway director, but also master of foxhounds and captain of the local yeomanry. These local connections were important in the success of an official. When an appointment was unsuccessful it was usually because he was opposed by men of such social mettle.

The new inspectorate

At this sort of level, offering £1,000 per annum plus expenses, it was not so difficult to find men of sufficient calibre as at the lower levels. At these levels in administration it was a challenge to find the numbers of men needed who were literate, sober, hardworking and honest. The records of the early work of the factory inspectorate show this for the levels below the factory inspectors themselves. From the beginning in 1833 the inspectors were assisted by junior officials called superintendents (later sub-inspectors). There was repeated trouble in the first 20 years of the inspectorate, sometimes because of incompetence, sometimes because of incapacity. But there are more sinister examples, such as the career of James Webster, who not only showed a disinclination to move from his home in Bath to inspect any factories, but also, from the degrees of his indebtedness to factory owners, attracted more than a suspicion of corruption.

Within the Poor Law system there was a flow of drunken or inefficient relieving officials, absconding collectors of rates and embezzling workhouse masters in the years after 1834. Probably the new system was better at weeding them out than the old one had been. We have had an inherent bias in our evidence, which is a general tendency in historical evidence, to pay more attention to things which have gone badly than to things which have gone well. The fact that about 10% of

Poor Law officers were got rid of in the 10 years after 1834 could however be taken as a sign of success, not of failure. This is not necessarily how it was seen by the ratepayers who funded the system. It is well to remember that throughout the nineteenth century and for some time afterwards, the money for the relief of the poor came directly from the local ratepayers, in what were then still coherent, and often small communities. There was thus a good chance that the ratepayers would know the people to whom their money was being given. This could sometimes be a recipe for generosity, but was just as likely to generate hostility towards those who were known, in some cases, to be the undeserving poor. This particular arrangement for the relief of the poor thus had social, as well as fiscal, significance.

It is easy for us to see the history of nineteenth-century Britain in a wide perspective of history. For the people who held responsible positions in that society it was not easy. They had to respond to a society which was changing with unprecedented rapidity with an extremely feeble array of administrative resources. Much of what was done both in legislation and administration was experimental. I refer any student who believes in *laissez-faire* in the nineteenth century to the Merchant Shipping Act of 1850.

There was also a learning process for legislators. In 1850 the government realised that the inspection of mines could not be left to well-meaning amateurs, but people who knew about mines would have to be appointed. In the North East they appointed the mining engineer, Matthias Dunn. In his letter of appointment he was charged:

> You will bear in mind the confidential nature of some of the information which you may acquire, and you will carefully guard against any violation of secrecy. You will not fail to act with courtesy and forbearance in your official intercourse with all parties and you will encourage a good feeling between the miners and their employers. Although it will not fall within your province to take any direct measures for promoting education among the miners you may usefully avail yourself of any opportunity of pointing out to them the importance of education and you may lay your influence to the encouragement of any well-devised plan for advancing their moral and intellectual development. The district assigned to you [remember the quality of transport and communications in 1850] will for the present comprise the counties of Durham, Northumberland, Cumberland and the adjoining districts of Scotland.

I want to cite just two more examples of administrative procedures in these years. We think of the Municipal Reform Act of 1835 as a good example of statutory reform preceded by a Royal Commission

Inquiry. In fact it was not like that at all. The Royal Commission was packed with those who were already committed to a particular view of reform. The well-paid patronage 'perk' of secretary to the Royal Commission was given to the Whig government's principal election agent, Joseph Parkes, who was soon in confidential correspondence with opposition groups within the existing boroughs. The resultant Municipal Reform Act of 1835 provided a reformed kind of urban local government. In some cases at least, including Newcastle upon Tyne, the reformed council, elected by the ratepayers, was much more reluctant to spend on schemes of town improvement than their unreformed predecessors had been.

The second example is the factory legislation of 1833 and 1844. One of the principal features of this legislation was, as was also the case with the Mines Act 1842, the attempt to restrict the working hours of children. The practical problems facing those who had to implement the legislation was how to define a child. The legislation used age to define children. However, general registration of births, marriages and deaths had only begun in 1836, and for much of the population there was no precise way of telling their exact age. The legislators sought to deal with this problem by requiring surgeons to validate the age of a child. Quite apart from the imprecision this necessarily involved, it also raised the further problem of who, in early nineteenth-century Britain, could justly claim to be a surgeon. There was no agreed definition and no general register to which administrators could turn.

Such examples illustrate the difficulties faced by reformers and administrators in the early nineteenth century. In dealing with the social and industrial problems of a rapidly changing society they had to operate within the constraints that society imposed, the mores by which it functioned and the limitations which it involved. Despite the ebullient expansionism of British commerce in this period, these limitations were very real. All reforms require for their implementation the requisite administrative tools, which in this period often had to be forged in a rough and ready fashion by a process of trial and error. It is important to bear in mind that such considerations both affected the possibility of reform and necessarily shaped its course and outcome.

Norman McCord is Emeritus Professor of Social History, University of Newcastle upon Tyne.

Peter Mandler
The New Poor Law

Was the New Poor Law a Benthamite measure or a vehicle of landed control?
Peter Mandler examines the debate.

Every generation writes its own New Poor Law. The 1834 Act encompassed such a wide range of interests, and had such multiple and contradictory effects upon politics, society and economy that it cannot easily be summed up under any one interpretation. Accordingly we tend to see in it what we are looking for, and we look for different things at different periods. This does not mean that scholarship is in vain, always bound to be overwhelmed by our contemporary concerns. After all, later interpretations cannot exactly ignore earlier ones; they must be faced and integrated somehow. But it does mean that we have to take frequent stock of the historiography of the New Poor Law – the layers of interpretation that have been built up over time – if we are to make fresh contributions. If nothing else, such a stock-taking provides a salutary reminder that the past is just as rich and variegated as the present: it is only our representations of it that are simple.

The liberal view

For a long time, the study of both the origins and the operation of the New Poor Law was dominated by the idea of Benthamism. A small corps of rather low-born liberals, acolytes of the visionary Jeremy Bentham, were thought to have infiltrated themselves into the corrupt and aristocratic machinery of government after 1832 and adapted it to modern industrial conditions. In the case of the Poor Law, this meant sweeping away entirely the old system of individual parish autonomy, run in an amateurish fashion by lazily paternalist magistrates and easily intimidated parish overseers. In their place was put a nationally uniform system overseen by a Poor Law Commission in London, with key positions reserved for Benthamites. The policy they imposed was dictated by strict classical political economy, which insisted that those who did not labour should not be permitted a standard of living more luxurious – more 'eligible' – than the worst-paid labour. This 'less eligibility' principle was enforced by applying the workhouse test, by which relief was only dispensed to those who would enter workhouses purposely built to intimidate and deter, the notorious 'Poor Law Bastilles'.

At the heart of this programme lay an interesting contradiction: in order to impose the rules of classical political economy, the rules of *laissez-faire* which were supposed to arise naturally in a market economy, a tremendously authoritarian bureaucracy had first to be set up. Assistant Commissioners had to scurry about the country forbidding local landowners to run their own relief policies and forcing them to build expensive workhouses instead. Central Commissioners had to be established in London – at a time when the central administration employed only a handful of officers – to oversee the new system. Diets, workhouse plans, the appointment of workhouse masters and auditors, the election of local guardians to administer the new scheme: all had to be scrutinised from the centre.

This contradiction did not bother the early historians of the New Poor Law, in large part because of the heroic role assigned to the Benthamites. To late Victorian and early twentieth-century historians, who felt that in many ways they still lived in an aristocratic society, the Benthamites appeared to be glorious professional shock troops who had made an early and pioneering breach in the aristocratic system. If they had to adopt unusual methods – if personally they seemed overzealous and even eccentric – it was all ultimately in the cause of individual liberty. In its subtlest form, this liberal version of the New Poor Law appears in the works of the French historian Elie Halévy, which began to appear just before the First World War.[1]

The Fabian view

This tradition of exaggerating the Benthamites' role was perpetuated between the World Wars and beyond by a new generation of historians inspired by Fabian socialism. Sidney and Beatrice Webb laid the foundation for this Fabian history, with a magnificent multi-volume history of the Poor Laws (1927–29) that laid emphasis on the Benthamites' administrative innovations.[2] The Webbs, socialists and would-be bureaucrats themselves, reversed the liberal view by seeing the New Poor Law not as an unfortunately interventionist means to a sound liberal-individualist end, but rather as a contribution to the growth of the central state, which temporarily followed evil liberal-individualist principles. In the new view, Chadwick and the Benthamites were no longer characteristic figures of the age of individualism, but rather pioneers of the Fabians' own social conscience – or sometimes both! For in this literature, angry socialist denunciations of post-1834 relief practices – 'social fascism' was one epithet employed – could sit bizarrely side by side with paeans of praise to the great Benthamite democrats and social reformers who helped excite the modern social conscience. Overall the heroic, biographical focus continued to dominate, and we owe to Fabian influence (direct or indirect) no fewer than three biographies of Chadwick. The greatest of these –

The Life and Times by S.E. Finer, begun before the Second World War but not published until 1952 – still provides the definitive portrait of that 'intolerant, precipitate, surly, humourless, opinionated' man who nevertheless had 'a passion for public causes ... original, daring, ardent, and indomitable'.[3]

The Poor Law and the Welfare State

After the Second World War, at a time when the modern state was being dramatically expanded, studies of social policy and its history became more sophisticated. Though the Fabian view remained dominant, the heroic and biographical approach gave way to more systematic inquiries. In the 1960s, for instance, the famous 'Victorian Revolution in government' controversy put forward several different models to explain why state intervention had extended since the early nineteenth century. Some authors, notably Henry Parris and Jennifer Hart, insisted on the role of ideology and the contribution of the Benthamites; others, like Oliver MacDonagh, saw government growth as a natural function of a broader process of modernisation that came inevitably with urbanisation and industrialisation. In this debate, the New Poor Law played a surprisingly marginal role, probably because its *laissez-faire* features put off historians seeking the 'Victorian origins of the modern welfare state'. They focused instead on topics as disparate as railway regulation, factory and public health legislation and the promotion of emigration.[4]

Meanwhile, the more systematic study of welfare policy did shed some new light on the Poor Law, in other ways. The general tendency was to cut down to size the more extravagant claims made both for the 1834 Act itself and for the Benthamites' achievement made by liberals and Fabians. The most important contribution came from an economist, Mark Blaug, who was the first to challenge directly the diagnosis of the Old Poor Law made by the Benthamite authors of the New Poor Law. In key articles published in 1963 and 1964, Blaug argued that the allowances offered under the Old Poor Law had not been corrupt and excessive, did not act to reduce wages or stimulate population growth, but were rather a rational response to structural changes in the economy that might otherwise have led to social unrest. He accused the Benthamites of 'fixing' the evidence in the famous Poor Law Report of 1834 and historians for taking that evidence on faith. In practice, he thought, local Poor Law administrators were always able to adjust relief policies to meet local needs: this was easier before 1834 (and he found considerable evidence for non-doctrinaire reforms of corrupt practices in the 1820s), but continued in spite of the best efforts of the Poor Law Commissioners to impose the new principles.[5]

This last point offered an opening for local historians, who were also enjoying something of a heyday in the 1960s and 1970s. Most confirmed Blaug's suspicion that the Old Poor Law was not so bad and the New Poor Law not so new. Substantial continuities between the old and new laws were noted. Above all, a tremendous diversity of practice was asserted against the propaganda of Benthamites and Bethamite historians. Attention shifted from the central apparatus of Poor Law administration, so beloved of the Fabians, to the Boards of Guardians, elected by ratepayers at the local level, who carried out the scheme. In the rural districts for which the New Poor Law was designed, these Guardians, it was pointed out, were principally landlords with traditional if not paternalist attitudes to their dependents. Beneath them lay the farmers, the direct employers of labour. Between these two forces, it was argued, the true day-to-day struggle over relief policy was conducted, determined not by central diktat but by custom, changing labour market conditions, and face-to-face social relations.[6] A predictable cap to these arguments came in the form of a 1978 book by Anthony Brundage, which aimed to demonstrate that the 1834 Act itself was the creation of landlords who used it to consolidate their local position against farmers and labourers.[7]

The Poor Law and society

Today most historians would, I think, consider this worm's-eye view of the New Poor Law to be just as one-sided as the old Fabian bird's-eye view. The Benthamites did not create an all-powerful centralised state overnight in 1834, but neither were local authorities any longer as independent in the conduct of their relief policy as they had been under the old regime. The benefit of these historians' debates has been to force us to consider the New Poor Law as a part of society as a whole, not an administrative mechanism which can be examined on its own, but not a matter for insulated rural authorities to settle amongst themselves either. To see the New Poor Law in this way requires a longer-term perspective, if we are not to get tangled up in the complexities of the moment. Let me, finally, point to a few of these longer-term perspectives, as evident in recent writing on the New Poor Law, without imagining that this recent literature is any more definitive than what came before it.

First, it seems clear that the 1834 Act *did* play a role in a great transformation of the English countryside, if not the towns. If we look at the *aggregate* national statistics, lumping together all the local variations, it appears that the number of able-bodied men – labourers capable of employment – in receipt of poor relief dropped dramatically after 1834. The workhouse did deter these unemployed men from accepting poor relief. Where flexibility and relative generosity remained was in the sphere of the aged and infirm, and there was indeed substantial continuity in the number of aged and infirm people (proportionate to the population) in receipt of poor relief over the course of the nineteenth century.[8] This kind of analysis – as well as other work stressing the psychological and cultural impact of the workhouse's very presence on the rural population – has tended to restore belief in the New Poor Law as a socially and economically decisive piece of legislation.

But has it restored belief in the Benthamites? Here there remains ground for doubt. In political history the trend has been to play down the influence of anti-aristocratic, radical middle-class elements in nineteenth-century governance. The local historians are surely right to regard Poor Law administration as a quintessentially landed affair. To bring together these perspectives, Boyd Hilton and I have tried to show how landlords themselves had both an economic interest and an ideological belief in a New Poor Law that would bring less paternalist, more individualist social relations to the countryside.[9] The great English landlords were no reactionary backwoodsmen: they were the best-educated and best-connected figures in the land, with interests in science as well as religion, technology as well as the arts, central administration as well as local government. By the 1820s, their political leaders had been very largely converted to a kind of capitalist individualism. This was not the radical, democratic individualism of a Benthamite, but a more puritan individualism shaped by a belief in Christian discipline, the naturalness of the social hierarchy, and by low expectations of social and economic change. These Christian individualists preached hard work and sacrifice not so much because they expected an industrial revolution and personal liberation to result, as because they feared divine retribution and economic failure if virtue was not performed. On this basis, cautious landed politicians like Sir Robert Peel and Lord Althorp could co-operate with Benthamites like Chadwick in struggling against paternalism and local laxity, but with very different social philosophies. One key difference was that few politicians saw the central apparatus as a permanent tool for social improvement – the origins of a Welfare State – where Benthamites did. It was possible for some people to view the Poor Law Commission as a temporary expedient, while others saw it as the nucleus of an expanding bureaucracy.[10]

This approach has the healthy effect of reconnecting administrative and social history, town and country, London and the provinces. The landed politicians who directed administrative reforms from the centre were often the same people who, as magistrates and guardians, enforced them in the country. Their belief in a stricter individualism had to be fought for locally against labourers' resistance, the traditionalism of the parish clergy, and the economic interests of farmers (who had used the Old Poor Law to subsidise their wage bill – often, said the landlords, at their expense). But this was a division within the landed community and not a town *vs* country issue.

We can now see the origins of the New Poor Law as something more than the Benthamites' victory over aristocratic paternalism. We can see it as involving a whole range of overlapping conflicts: labourers *vs* farmers, farmers *vs* landlords, individualist landlords *vs* traditionalist landlords, Christian individualists *vs* radical individualists. The whole of society comes into play. Of course, putting all these different factors into the equation only gives historians more scope for picking and choosing what they want to see and emphasise, angling their representations of history in the light of the present. But that is a process that will never end, not as long as historians remain citizens of the present as well as of the past.

Notes

(1)   Halevy, E. *The Liberal Awakening 1815–30* and *The Triumph of Reform 1830–41*, Vols II and III of his *History of the English People in the Nineteenth Century* (first published in French in 1912).
(2)   Webb, S. and Webb, B. *English Poor Law History*, 3 Vols. (Longman, 1927–29), forming Vols VII–IX of their *English Local Government.*
(3)   Finer, S. E. *The Life and Times of Sir Edwin Chadwick* (Methuen, 1952).
(4)   Important contributions to this debate are collected in Stansky, P. (ed.) *The Victorian Revolution* (New Viewpoints, 1973).
(5)   Blaug, M. 'The myth of the Old Poor Law and the making of the New' and 'The Poor Law Report re-examined', *Journal of Economic History* 23 (1963) and 24 (1964).
(6)   A useful summary of the first stage of this research can be found in Digby, A. 'Recent developments in the study of the English Poor Law', *The Local Historian* 12 (1976–77).
(7)   Brundage, A. *The Making of the New Poor Law 1832–39* (Hutchinson, 1978).
(8)   Williams, K. *From Pauperism to Poverty* (Routledge and Kegan Paul, 1981).
(9)   Hilton, B. *The Age of Atonement* (Oxford University Press, 1988). Mandler, P. *Aristocratic Government in the Age of Reform* (Oxford University Press, 1990).
(10)   Mandler, P. 'The making of the New Poor Law *Redivivus*', *Past and Present* 117 (1987), with responses from A. Brundage and D. Eastwood in *Past and Present* 127 (1990).

Peter Mandler is Senior Lecturer in Modern History at London Guildhall University.

Hugh Cunningham
The Nature of Chartism

Hugh Cunningham reinterprets the nature of the Chartist movement in Britain in the 1830s and 1840s, and the causes of its subsequent decline.

Chartism has been the subject of considerable debate over the past decade, leading to a reconsideration of the orthodoxy which was established in the 1950s and 1960s. In that earlier perspective, Chartism was seen as a movement of a working class which in a variety of ways was too immature to sustain itself. All but one of the six constitutional points of the Charter were eventually to be enacted, but none of them in the lifetime of Chartism itself. Chartism therefore came to be thought of as a perhaps inevitable, perhaps noble failure.

It was not difficult, within this perspective, to accumulate a significant number of causes of failure. Chartism, it was said, was an economic cause masquerading as a political one, and it had strength only when economic conditions were bad, in the late 1830s, in 1842 and in 1848. Once economic conditions improved, Chartism faded away.

In so far as it was a political movement, Chartism was seen as a product of the disenchantment between the working classes and the Whig government after 1832. The Reform Act of 1832, which gave the vote to the middle but not to the working classes, was followed by a succession of measures which might have been designed to alienate any remaining working-class goodwill. They included the 1833 Irish Coercion Act (there were links between Irish nationalists and British radicals, and it was feared that coercion thought suitable for the Irish might soon be applied on the mainland); the 1833 Factory Act, a government measure which deliberately set aside vociferous demands for a ten hour day; the 1834 transportation of the Tolpuddle martyrs with its attack on the rights of trade unionists; the 1835 Act which allowed boroughs to set up their own police forces, for the police were seen as quite alien to British traditions of freedom; and above all, the passage and implementation of the Poor Law Amendment Act of 1834. These government measures called forth a massive degree of resistance which was to culminate in the publication of the People's Charter, the organisation for the first National Petition, and the elections for the first Convention. But, as with the economy, it was argued that once the conditions which had given rise to Chartism were removed, Chartism itself disintegrated.

For the Chartists, it was said, could not call on a united working class; their support came from disparate groups with different objectives; the handloom weavers in a declining trade had little in common with factory workers or with skilled artisans, and the chances of these three groups acting in unison were slim. Furthermore, it was claimed that Chartism could be understood only in a local, not a national context; in different towns and regions people calling themselves Chartists had quite different objectives, and quite different means of advancing their cause. Nothing but the name of Chartist held together the Christian Chartists of Scotland and the advanced thinkers of the East London Democratic Federation. All these differences were reflected in a divided leadership and conflicting strategies. Moral force was counterpoised to physical force, the difference for most students being embodied in the persons of William Lovett and Feargus O'Connor; the latter, indeed, with his rhetoric of physical force, his ambition, his diversionary land plan, and his ultimate insanity was often credited with much of the blame for the failure of Chartism.

These 'causes of failure' could be and often were expanded to fill a whole essay. From the moment of its inception, Chartism was seen as in decline, hastening towards its doom. In some accounts, there was not much to be said for Chartism after the winter of 1839–40; the two later peaks in 1842 and 1848 were treated as mere repetitive epilogues, and the survival of Chartism into the 1850s was written out of the script. All this, explicitly or implicitly, stood in marked contrast with the 'success' of the middle-class Anti-Corn Law League, for the Corn Laws were repealed in 1846. Modern historians would not attribute repeal entirely or even mainly to the activities of the League, but it was easy to draw the conclusion that success in politics in the 1840s lay with these middle-class, well-organised, and single issue pressure groups, rather than with attempts to mobilise the masses on behalf of what would have amounted to a revolution in the political system.

The tradition of radical politics

A fuller understanding of Chartism requires a longer historical perspective. In organising resistance to the government in the 1830s, the Chartists were able to draw on a tradition of popular radicalism which dated back at least as far as John Wilkes in the 1760s. At the heart of that radicalism lay a sense of history. The publication and immense popularity of Tom Paine's *The Rights of Man* had enabled people since the 1790s to base their political demands on natural rights, but British radicals simply added this new weapon to their existing armoury, which was rooted in the belief that before the Norman Conquest there had been a democratic constitution in Britain. British history since 1066 was interpreted as a series of attempts to bring back democracy, for example at the time of Magna Carta, or in the great struggles of the seventeenth century. Radicals described themselves as 'patriots', as people devoted to the true interests of their country, in contrast to a government which was the embodiment of 'corruption'. 'Old Corruption' was the name William Cobbett and others gave to the British state.

This kind of thinking was deeply embedded in Chartism and its precursors. In the campaign for shorter hours of work, some radicals demanded an eight hour day on the grounds that good King Alfred had divided the 24 hours into eight for work, eight for sleep and eight for recreation. The name 'Alfred' adorned the titles of campaigning newspapers. Food and drink – roast beef, plum pudding, and beer – were further symbols of the times which had once existed and which ought to be restored. Historians have made much of the speech which Joseph Rayner Stephens delivered at Kersal Moor outside Manchester in September 1838, when he said that Chartism was 'a knife-and-fork question'. They have also chuckled condescendingly at the Chartist of Trowbridge in Wiltshire who promised his audience that if the Charter was enacted there would be 'plenty of roast beef, plum pudding and strong beer by working three hours a day'. The implication is that Chartism appealed to people's bellies and not their reason, and that in a place like Trowbridge people had no real understanding of democratic politics. The symbolic language of food, however, pervades all sections of Chartism. George Julian Harney, often taken as representative of the left wing of Chartism, demanded universal suffrage in a speech in 1839 'because it is our right, and not only because it is our right, but because we believe it will bring freedom to our country and happiness to our homesteads; we believe it will give us bread and beer and beef'. In August 1840 at a great banquet in the Manchester Hall of Science, held to celebrate the release from prison of two Chartists, the band played 'Oh, the roast beef of Old England', and on the menu were plum puddings – for which there was 'a bit of a scramble'.

The six points of the Charter, then, were part of a political programme which dated back to the eighteenth century and which, if enacted, would bring an end to 'Old Corruption', and restore the long-eroded birthrights of Britons. To assist in this restoration the Chartists insisted on another right, the right to bear arms. Harney had continued his speech by reminding his audience that

time was when every Englishman had a musket in his cottage, and along with it hung a flitch of bacon; now there was no flitch of bacon for there was no musket; let the musket be restored and the flitch of bacon would soon follow.

This could easily be categorized as a 'physical force' speech. But every section of Chartism insisted on this right to bear arms. The moderate newspaper, *The Chartist*, argued that 'recourse to physical force to free themselves from an unendurable tyranny' is, for Englishmen, 'the very foundation of our system of government', and it urged its readers to 'retain your arms then, for it is possible that you may have to use them in your own defence, with the law and the constitution upon your side'. So deeply imbued were Chartists with the notion that the state was corrupt, that they saw themselves as defenders of the constitution, fighting, if fight they must, under the watchwords of 'Peace, Law, Order' – a phrase used approvingly by both Harney and *The Chartist*.

Chartism and the economy

It is only by understanding the elements that went into the making of Chartism that we can begin to grasp the causes of its decline. They are more complex than the simple emphasis on the movement's vulnerability to improvements in the economy. For the mid-Victorian boom, on which this argument leans, turns out to be something of a myth. Economic historians of the period from 1850 to 1873 now argue that the economy remained as unstable in that period as in the preceding 20 years, and that such a rise in living standards as occurred was concentrated almost exclusively in the late 1860s and early 1870s; the pattern of slump and boom continued, with particularly bad slumps in 1858 and 1866, providing fertile breeding ground for a movement such as Chartism had been – but was no longer. In 8 out of the 14 years between 1851 and 1864 real wages were at or below the level of 1850. The straightforward economic explanation of the decline of Chartism begins to look less than convincing.

It is possible, of course, that there may have been more complex changes in the economy which affected the viability of Chartism. Certainly the boom in railway building, with the stimulus which it gave to the iron, steel and coal industries, helped to stabilise capitalism and to give it a broader base than the textile industry. At the same time employers began to introduce new management techniques based on an acceptance of shorter hours of work; the 1847 Ten Hours Act may be said to mark this point. Thereafter, employers aimed to increase productivity within working hours by giving some workers the authority to act as pacemakers.

In the early 1970s and early 1980s it was frequently argued that these changes had led to the emergence by mid-century of a 'labour aristocracy' consisting of some 10 or 15% of the workers who were cut off from the rest by superior wages and better working conditions. Such people might in other circumstances have provided the leadership for a working-class movement, but as it was, it was argued, they tended to see things through their employers' eyes. Few historians would now endorse this view of the importance of a 'labour aristocracy'. In practice it proved difficult to identify labour aristocrats, and often, when identified, they turned out to be more radical than one might have expected. Even a relatively sophisticated economic explanation for the decline of Chartism leaves many issues unresolved.

Chartists and politics

In these circumstances historians have turned to more political explanations. Chartism, as we have seen, arose out of a long political tradition; within that tradition there was not only a common set of political presuppositions, but also an agreement on the strategies to be employed in the face of 'Old Corruption'. If the people could be assembled in big enough masses, it was argued, the government would be forced to concede. There were various ways in which what we would now call 'people power' could be demonstrated. Petitions, signed by millions, and presented to Parliament by a sympathetic MP, had a long history as a means of presenting a grievance. In Chartist times they were backed up by mass public meetings. Chartism indeed, in this perspective, was not a series of local campaigns, but emphatically a national one. Its petitions were national in scope; in the *Northern Star* it had a national newspaper, selling at its height 50,000 copies, and perhaps reaching one million readers or listeners – for it was often read aloud. In the National Charter Association with its 400 localities and 50,000 members, it had what was arguably the first national political organisation. Finally, in Feargus O'Connor, the inspiration of the National Charter Association, it had a national leader. As a national movement, Chartists believed it legitimate to call a duly elected anti-parliament, a convention, supposedly more representative of the people than the partliament which sat at Westminster.

Such was Chartism at its height. But there were two difficulties which such a strategy of mass mobilisation always faced. The first was that parliament and government would simply refuse to accept 'people power' at face value; that they would reject the petitions and mock them. If that happened, what were the Chartists to do? It was this issue which led inevitably to divisions, with some supporting an armed uprising, others talking of a national strike in the form of a 'sacred month', and others more cautiously recommending a re-consideration of tactics. The second potential difficulty was that the government would meet the Chartists on their own ground, and to the Chartist numbers counterpoise their own. This was what happened on 10 April 1848 at Kennington Common; the Chartists who wished to present their petition were confronted in London by 7,000 soldiers, 4,000 police and 85,000 special constables sworn in for the occasion. As one contemporary put it, the Chartists 'made number their argument and it recoiled upon themselves'.

The 'fiasco' of Kennington Common in 1848 is seen by many as the end of Chartism. It did indeed mark the end of the tactic of the 'mass platform', the attempt to gain Chartist ends by sheer force of numbers. Thereafter Chartists resorted either to conspiracy, or, as many had already done, to a policy of mutual self-improvement which would eventually convince the governing classes that working men could be admitted to the vote.

The role of the state

The resort to a more quietist politics reflected two somewhat contradictory trends of the 1840s. The first was that Chartists of all kinds had been brought face to face with the sheer power of the state. Twenty people had died in the Newport rising of November 1839. Over 500 Chartists, including Lovett, had been 'detained' between June 1839 and June 1840. To be an active Chartist was to be at constant risk of imprisonment. Not surprisingly, this affected the ability of the movement to sustain itself; many Chartists fled to America, to what they saw as a freer political climate.

But alongside this repressive side of state action lay something which historians increasingly call 'the liberalisation of the state'. In one sense this simply meant cleaning up 'Old Corruption' – doing away with of jobs for which people had been paid taxpayers' money without doing very much in return. More positively, the government, particularly under the premiership of Sir Robert Peel between 1841 and 1846, began to govern in what seemed to be the interests of the people as a whole. Taxes on consumption were reduced; the Coal Mines Act of 1842 and the Ten Hours Act of 1847 did seem to offer protection to some categories of workers; there was some state money made available for education and for public libraries. Peel himself was seen to be a 'statesman' rather than a mere 'politician', and it became increasingly difficult to think of the state as 'Old Corruption'.

Chartism found it hard to operate in this new political climate. The language which it had inherited from the radical tradition had lost its relevance. By the late 1840s those who talked about roast beef, or the Anglo-Saxon constitution, or the Englishman's right to bear arms, seemed to belong to an age that had passed. Chartism indeed is better seen as an end than a beginning. It brought to a head the eighteenth-century radical conception of the oppositional relationship between the people and the state. Once the state had transformed itself by a combination of repression and reform, Chartism no longer had a role to play. It attempted in the late 1840s and 1850s to build itself a new language of socialism, but did so without anything approaching the mass support it had enjoyed in the late 1830s and early 1840s. For at its height Chartism had support from all sectors of the working class, and from many small tradesmen and shopkeepers. To be linked with the six points of the Charter was to be part of a movement which asserted the power of the people against the state.

The end of Chartism

It is possible to trace connections between Chartism and later movements for political representation. Some Chartists ended up on the radical wing of Gladstone's Liberal Party; others, in Lancashire, carried on a tradition of Tory Radicalism in which the Liberal factory owners were the enemy; others still can be linked to the socialist politics of the 1880s. In time five of the Charter's six points were to become part of the law of the land. But it is only hindsight, with its attendant dangers, which permits us to trace these links with the future. The five points were achieved not *because* the Chartists had voiced them; rather, they were conceded by a state which had defeated Chartism and which no longer felt threatened. After 1848 the fear of revolution receded sharply in Britain. New dangers came to confront the state. There is no clearer sign of the new mood of politics, and of the way in which Chartism had been consigned to the past, than the emergence in 1859–60 of a Volunteer Force to defend Britain's shores against French invasion; most of its members were working class, and they enjoyed the privilege of taking their rifles home with them. One of the Chartists' demands had been met, but the government could now be confident that the arms were for use against an external enemy rather than the state itself. The Chartist age was over.

Further Reading

Briggs, A. (ed.) *Chartist Studies* (Macmillan, 1962).

Epstein, J. and Thompson, D. (eds) *The Chartist Experience* (Macmillan, 1982).

Epstein, J. *The Lion of Freedom: Feargus O'Connor and the Chartist Movement 1832–1842* (Croom Helm, 1982).

Jones, D. J. V. *Chartism and the Chartists* (Lane, 1975).

Mather, F. C. *Chartism and Society* (Bell & Hyman 1980).

Royle, E. *Chartism* (Longman, 1980).

Saville, J. *1848: The British State and the Chartist Movement* (Cambridge University Press, 1987).

Thompson, D. *The Chartists* (Temple Smith, 1984).

Hugh Cunningham is Senior Lecturer in History at the University of Kent.

Tim Chapman
Ireland 1800–50:
John Bull's Other Island

Why was Ireland such a central issue in British politics in the first half of the nineteenth century, and why did its problems prove so intractable?

Between the Act of Union in 1801 and the Great Famine of the 1840s, Ireland played a central, even pivotal, part in British history. This, however, was never meant to be the case; Ireland was subject to a series of 'quick fixes' granted with reluctance to shore up the mainland's safety and security. Successive leaders took a national, i.e. Anglocentric, view rather than a party political one and where party differences arose they hinged on the most appropriate method of control. From the highest point in London, Ireland was seen above all as a strategic matter, as a potential base for foreign attack; any other considerations were secondary to this.

The Union

The government in Westminster had good reasons for thinking in this way, for over the centuries Ireland had proved to be the friend of English enemies. As far back as 1690, Ireland had supported the Catholic King James II against the strongly Protestant Parliament. Likewise, the American colonies' rebellion in the 1770s led to Irish demands for better trading rights, and revolutionary France actively helped the Irish Rebellion of 1798. General Hoche landed at Bantry Bay in 1796 and General Humbert arrived with 1,000 men in County Mayo, just after the uprising had been crushed.

It was this last rebellion that led to the Act of Union being passed. Pitt the Younger, as Prime Minister, at first tried to preserve the status quo. Ireland had its own Parliament which was nominally independent; in practice, the country was still ruled indirectly by Britain through various forms of patronage, which were used to ensure the 300-strong assembly followed London's bidding. Under this system Catholics were granted more freedoms, including the right to vote, but problems arose over finance. Dublin was virtually bankrupt in 1796 and had to be bailed out by Britain. When Dublin also failed to quell the activities of Wolfe Tone's Society of United Irishmen, which organised the 1798 rebellion, Pitt felt compelled to impose direct rule. Patronage was used again to push the Act of Union through the Irish

Parliament, and in all, over £1.5 million was spent in this way. Under its terms, Ireland was represented by 100 elected MPs in London, together with 28 temporal and 4 spiritual peers.[1] This arrangement took two years to achieve, but it had been slowed by the initial hostility of the Irish Parliament. In order to speed up the process, issues that London thought subsidiary were separated out. Thus, Catholic emancipation was promised but not passed. The urgent strategic problem had been settled and this was London's overriding aim. Direct rule implied firmer maintenance of order, properly financed, and while it was King George III who vetoed emancipation in 1801 (rather than Parliament) no English minister cared to take up the Catholic cause until almost 30 years later.

The island that was now part of the United Kingdom was a very difficult place to govern. It may have been for this reason that in the eighteenth century Britain preferred to have a strong influence over Ireland, rather than full governmental responsibility for it. The problems were profound, but they were partly of Britain's own making. Certainly they deserved more attention than was given them by the British Parliament. The problems involved the economy and especially land, the churches, violence and Irish Nationalism, which focused on emancipation in the 1820s and repeal of the Act of Union in the 1840s.

Society

In trying to understand these problems, it is important first to appreciate the nature of Irish society during this period. It was universally poor and Catholic. About 80% of the population belonged to the Catholic Church, the established Church of Ireland (which was Anglican) attracted 10% of Irish people to its services and the various Presbyterian churches (which were of Scottish origin) had almost as many. The latter two were Protestant and were based mainly in the north, although as the established church, the Church of Ireland, drew tithes from the entire population.

Ireland as a whole was not particularly poor, but the distribution of wealth was severely imbalanced, with most land concentrated in the hands of an aristocratic Protestant élites. Some 10,000 landowners had estates, but many of these were absent for much of the year and knew little about what went on. In 1846, one lord who had originally let his land at 10 shillings an acre to 60 tenants discovered that after sub-letting, his land was worth £1 10s for a quarter of an acre and he had 600 tenants. Farming was not carried out by the landowners; normally there was a middleman or agent who negotiated the leasing of farms. Farmers usually had from 15–100 acres of rented land and, depending on the size of their holding, were described as family farmers, 'snug' farmers or rich farmers. They accounted for no more than a quarter of the population and numbered perhaps 400,000 adult males. The vast bulk of the population were labourers (i.e. peasants) who rented less than five acres apiece, and quite possibly none at all. This class incorporated 80% of Irish society, living in poverty. In 1841, 40% of the houses in Ireland were one-roomed mud cabins, and in 1838 the commissioners who were sent out to assess how to apply the Poor Law to Ireland concluded that the country was so poor that the workhouse system would just not work.

Agriculture

This sorry state was partly the result of periodic shifts in the ownership of land brought about for English political reasons. In 1610, Catholics held two-thirds of the land; by 1690, Protestants held almost 80% of the land as a result of the conquests of Cromwell in the 1640s and the defeat of James II in 1690. Subsequent legislation, the Penal Laws, discriminated against Catholics and although this was applied with varying degrees of severity, their share of the land had fallen to 7% by 1750. Primogeniture was abolished for Catholics, so many holdings they kept were badly fragmented. Persecution became so intense that Catholics were banned from owning horses worth more than £5.

The experience of all classes of agricultural workers varied according to how well estates were run. Some were managed very badly; in 1844, 132 estates were in the hands of the courts, usually in preparation for paying off creditors. The better run estates were comparable in their efficiency with French farms at this time. However, there were powerful reasons for poor agricultural practices. Leases on land were normally very short, and unlikely to exceed three lives (i.e. the time taken for a holding to pass from grandfather to grandson). This discouraged investment by farmers who were uncertain of reaping the benefits of any long-term improvements and who were not entitled to compensation for anything they had done if they lost a farm after the expiry of the lease. One exception to this was the system operated in the northern counties, where the 'Ulster Tenant Right' meant there was remuneration for improvements.

Secondly, the wars against France had caused a general rise in prices from 1793 until 1815 and relative prosperity for Irish farmers. After the war, there was a fall in prices and a widespread depression in agriculture such that prices did not recover their 1815 level until the mid-1840s. To combat this, many landlords simply cancelled the existing leases and drew up new ones. These were often auctioned off to the highest bidder and existing farmers were left with no livelihood. This 'rack-renting' was common, and only possible because of the steadily growing pressure on land.

The Irish population was increasing at an extremely high rate, and although it tailed off in the 1820s and 1830s, it rose from about 2.5 million in 1750 to over 5 million in 1800 and to 8.25 million by 1845.[2] The desperation to have land to farm meant holdings were overpriced, restricting investment further. One contemporary remarked:

> ... [the negotiation of rents was] a commerce of extortion on one side and fraud on the other. One asks more than he knows he can get and the other offers more than he has any intention of paying.

The poorest members of society rented tiny pieces of land called conacre plots from farmers and used to cultivate potatoes because acre for acre, potatoes produced a bigger crop on which to support a family than any cereal could. Throughout this period, there was a virtual monoculture of potatoes for domestic consumption, while other crops were grown for cash and for export.

Commerce

While Britain industrialised before any other country in the world, Ireland's trading and manufacturing were retarded by the Navigation Acts, which treated Ireland as a colony until the 1770s. Any industry that rivalled one based in Britain was stifled, with the result that Ireland's economy became more dependent than ever on agriculture. The industries that did develop were mainly in the north (where Protestantism prevailed) and consisted of domestic textile production, particularly of linen, since there was no English rival. As Irish production changed from the putting-out system to factories in the 1830s, there were fewer jobs available to supplement agricultural workers' incomes and the dependence on potatoes grew.

Trading was possible for a number of ports, notably Belfast and Dublin and those towns along Ireland's south coast that supplied transatlantic shipping, such as Cork, which had a population of 80,000 in 1841. Commerce allowed the emergence of a Catholic as well as a Protestant middle class in Ireland from the middle of the eighteenth century. Both groups were loyal to mainland Britain up to and including the Act of Union. However, the failure to allow Catholics full rights as part of the United Kingdom after 1800 alienated this group and went on to divide the middle class along religious lines.

Protest

Violence and protest were endemic to Ireland and the forms they took before the Union also continued afterwards. The main motivation was by no means religion; most of the protests were caused by local problems, and attacks on property or livestock were generally carried out by the poor against the rich, whether they lived in Ulster or elsewhere. Thus, it was at times of distress that violence became most pronounced. In the aftermath of war and depression, the Carders of north Leinster (1813–16), the Rockites of Munster (1819–23) and men of Ribbonism were active; again, during the economic slump of 1828–32, there was unrest from the Whitefeet of Leinster (1830–34) and the Terry Alts of Clare (1831–32).

All of these groups were secret societies who acted after nightfall to carry out their attacks: hay ricks were burned, houses razed, shots were fired through windows and cattle were 'clifted' or driven over the edge of a cliff. The Carders' distinctive punishment was to draw a steel tooth comb through the flesh of their victim. Such measures were seen as breaches of the law by those with property, but to those who carried them out they were a form of community justice for crimes already committed by the wealthy. The roots of these reprisals lay with the 'Whiteboys' of the eighteenth century (so called because they blackened their faces, but wore white shirts for their activities).

These patterns of behaviour were not absolute, though. Violence broke out in the relatively prosperous war years before 1815, such as amongst the Threshers of Connaught, and it was also possible for middling farmers to organise themselves into vigilante groups. There was a bloody and bitter fight between snug farmers who called themselves Shanavests, and labourers who called themselves Caravats in Munster 1809–11. All of these groups had as their central concern everyday farming matters such as rents or the loss of conacre plots, which attracted only parochial interest; there were no national movements of this kind, and certainly nothing that could be described as nationalist, until O'Connell's campaign began. While Ireland was acknowledged by contemporaries to be a violent country, it was not in a constant state of unrest and upheaval: protest was sporadic, sudden and localised.

Religion

Land ownership rested heavily with the Protestant minority who controlled the country's estates and who received the large incomes these afforded, but who could not be relied upon to be resident in their manors and stately homes. Privilege was built into Irish life not just for the followers of Protestantism, but for the church itself. The Church of Ireland was financed by Catholics and Presbyterians, as well as by its own Anglican laity, through tithes which were compulsory church taxes worth about 10% of each year's production. Large parts of Ireland had no Protestant congregations, but the administrative structure of the Church of Ireland was in place as if it did. This meant there were too many Anglican ministers, in a church that had a perennial excess of income over expenditure of several hundred thousand pounds, paid for by an already impoverished peasantry. By contrast, there was a shortage of funds for the Catholic Church, which had difficulty finding enough priests for its masses. In 1800, there were barely 1,600 Roman Catholic priests in the entire country.

Beginnings of Reform

Given the enormity of Ireland's problems, it is not surprising that solutions were difficult to find. Furthermore, any British government that tried to deal with Ireland was faced with additional obstacles that related to the vagaries of mainland politics. In the years after 1800, the main Irish issue was Catholic emancipation (above all, whether or not to allow Catholics to sit in the British Parliament). Successive ministries were faced with a king, George III, who absolutely opposed emancipation on the grounds that it would break his coronation oath, and who threatened that the mere raising of the issue might induce the return of his ill-health. His views were supported eventually by Pitt the Younger, as well as by most Tories and those politicians who had any experience of Ireland – the past Lord Lieutenants, Lord Westmorland and Lord Camden. There was, therefore, a strong anti-emancipation group amongst Tory ministers.

By the time of Lord Liverpool's government (from 1812) the lines of division between Whig and Tory on emancipation were less clear, as Conservatives like Castlereagh and Canning favoured reform. The ministry was so badly split over what to do that it became an 'open' question – in other words, there was no policy at all. Ministers were free to vote with their conscience when the issue was debated in Parliament, but they themselves were not to initiate anything on the matter. Just as the Cabinet disagreed, equally there was a marked difference of opinion between the House of Commons and the electorate and wider mainland public. The Commons was always more sympathetic to emancipation and passed bills that would have allowed this on several occasions, including Plunkett's Bill (1821) and Nugent's Bill (1823). The electorate was suspicious of equal rights for Catholics and registered this at general elections (as in 1826) and the cry of 'No Popery' was still a popular one. The people were therefore closer in their attitude to the House of Lords, which rejected the Private Members' Bills on emancipation and consistently defended the Protestant constitution.

What then, could the government do? Faced with centuries of Protestant advantage in Ireland and a mainland population set in its anti-Catholic prejudice, there seemed to be few options. After 1815, precedence was given to matters such as tariff and legal reform, and whenever violence erupted in Ireland there was always the option of coercion. Acts of this kind were passed almost automatically, so as to suppress crimes rather than relieve their causes. However, a step towards reform was taken in 1814, when Peel as Chief Secretary passed the Peace Preservation Act. This set up a body of professional police and salaried magistrates in Dublin; the system was made national in 1822 and by 1837 it had 8,000 men. This showed concern for the problems, but it did not solve them and the violence continued.

O'Connell and emancipation

What broke the deadlock was a crisis engineered by a highly talented Catholic lawyer called Daniel O'Connell. He set up the Catholic Association in 1823 and enlisted the support of both the Catholic priests and the great mass of Irish Catholic peasants. By levying the 'Catholic Rent' of a penny a month on peasants and having it collected at the church door by the priests, O'Connell accumulated sufficient funds to mount a determined campaign for Catholic emancipation. Irish protest was no longer agrarian and local; it was now political and national. Political efforts in the past had been peaceful and limited to the middle classes; now, O'Connell made his appeals at outdoor meetings to secure broader support, and he co-ordinated activities so as to pressurise the British government into giving concessions. These methods were accompanied by electoral success in July 1828 when O'Connell himself was returned at a by-election as one of the two MPs for County Clare. He could not sit in the Commons, but he could make sure that at any future election the majority of Ireland's MPs were Catholic.

Wellington, the Prime Minister, recognised the danger and set about persuading those of his colleagues who were still hostile to emancipation that there was a need for it. Wellington's reasoning was there was a need for it. Peel, hitherto the leading opponent, realised the need to pass emancipation in order to preserve the Union, and both men were confirmed in their views by the reports of the Chief Secretary for Ireland. He warned that if peace was to be kept, then the Irish military budget needed to be radically increased. In the event, the act freeing Catholics was passed in just two months and opened up almost all official positions to them. So as to curtail the political danger from Ireland, the Irish county voting qualification was raised from 40 shillings to £10. This cut the number of voters from 216,000 to 37,000 and left the electorate almost wholly Protestant. The number of MPs that were followers of O'Connell never reached the levels initially feared and by 1841, the group had only 18 members.[3] The Act of Union had been passed quickly to prevent further unrest, and so was Catholic emancipation. Both were intended to keep Ireland quiet for the foreseeable future.

Whig policies in the 1830s

A change of government, however, brought something of a change of attitude. The Whigs had always been more favourable to emancipation than their Tory counterparts, and in the 1830s the Whig ministries tried to address some of the ecclesiastical problems. Irish schools were funded by the government from 1831 in a measure that foreshadowed the grant to English schools. The Irish Church Act of 1833 abolished 10 out of 22 sees and introduced a tax on clerical income to replace the unpopular church 'cess', an Easter tax. Problems arising from what to do with the Church of Ireland's surplus funds – whether to appropriate them to secular uses or not – led to the resignation of Grey and Melbourne's dismissal in 1834. The principles at stake seemed not to be Irish by nature, because Peel opposed appropriation as a tax on income; nevertheless, it was canny how he himself introduced income tax in the 1842 budget.

Peel's 'Hundred Days' were ended in 1835 by a coalition of the Whigs, Liberals and Irish in the Lichfield House Compact. This group saw the passage of further remedial measures; the 1838 Tithes Act commuted this tax to cash payments which ended the middling farmers' 'tithe war'.[4] The Irish Poor Law of 1838 led to the construction of over 100 workhouses and the 1840 Municipal Corporations Act was passed on almost identical lines to the English Act. Mention must also be made of the work of Thomas Drummond, Under-Secretary for Ireland 1835–40, who refused to rely on Coercion Acts and fostered instead a spirit of mutual trust between Catholics and Protestants. He encouraged the former to join the police force, and rebuked the latter's magistrates in Tipperary, pointing out that 'property has its duties as well as its rights'. These measures helped to relieve some of Ireland's problems, but there were no fundamental changes; the Church of Ireland was still intact and collecting revenue from Catholics and Presbyterians; the economy was still backward and most land remained in the same hands; and Ireland was still ruled from London, partly because O'Connell was ready to see what other reforms might be passed first. When the Whigs' hold on power failed he began to campaign once more, but this time to repeal the Union.

Peel's measures

Peel hoped to calm Ireland by winning over the Catholic priests and middle classes, so that the peasantry was deprived of leadership; this, he hoped, might also preserve the Union and the Church. To this end he increased the grant to St Patrick's College, Maynooth, where priests were trained for the Catholic Church, and he encouraged private funding of the Church through the Charitable Bequests Act. New university colleges were founded in Belfast, Cork and Galway. An attempt was also made to review the land issue in the form of a commission headed by Lord Devon. This goodwill on Peel's part was undermined from several directions. The Devon Commission reported in 1845, which turned out to be too late; a lot of government time was taken up with economic reforms for British industry, and dealing with O'Connell's campaign drained further resources. To these difficulties can be added the anger generated in his own party by the Maynooth Grant, and the split caused by the repeal of the Corn Law during the early stages of the Great Famine.

The significant changes in Ireland in the 1840s, then, were not of the government's making. O'Connell founded the Repeal Association in 1840, with the intention of using his 1828–29 tactics to demand more concessions. He raised the political temperature in Ireland with a series of outdoor meetings in 1841–43 which were to culminate at Clontarf. The year 1843 was dubbed 'repeal year'. Peel sent over extra troops, banned the meeting, and forced O'Connell to back down. O'Connell was arrested, jailed and fined. His threat to the Union was over, though the feelings that led to the campaign continued.

The government had little control over its own supporters in two key measures. The £26,000 Grant to Maynooth split the Conservative Party temporarily, with almost 150 of its MPs voting against the government. Of these, 108 also voted against the ending of the Corn Law. The end of protection for corn was entirely in line with the ministry's other free trade policies, but it seemed to threaten many Tory farmers' incomes and this caused their hostility. Peel had almost certainly chosen to repeal the Corn Law before 1846, but the timing was forced upon him by conditions in Ireland. Once again, it was the urgency of an Irish crisis that brought important change.

The famine

Local or regional famines had occurred in Ireland in previous decades, due to poor internal transport systems. Failures in the potato harvest led to relief measures in 1817, and there were shortages of food that left one million peasants destitute in 1822, and 300,000 in 1831. Again there were problems in 1835–37 and in 1842. The Great Famine of 1845–48 was much more severe, because the crop failures were in successive years and were far more widespread. Most of Europe's potatoes were blighted, so alternative sources of food were harder to find and the prices that shortages led to were beyond the means of most Irish people. The workhouses were entirely inadequate and unable to cope with mass starvation, and the government's relief attempts were insufficient – the Liberal government after 1846 tried to keep to a policy of non-intervention as best it could. Even so, by August 1847, three million people were being fed at makeshift soup kitchens, and charity for the able-bodied was allowed in breach of the Poor Law. Deaths that can be directly attributed to the famine amounted to something over one million and Ireland's population fell further, as emigration to England and America accounted for another one and a half million.

By 1850, Ireland was not much further forward than it had been in 1800. The Act of Union was still in force and land was still owned by absentee Protestants whose church was paid for (albeit in more palatable ways) mainly by non-members. The economy had advanced in some ways; factory production of textiles was well established, but agriculture remained relatively inefficient. The population was being decimated, and steadily declined from 8 million in 1845 to 4 million in 1916. Violence continued and the 1850s saw a series of Coercion Acts. Meanwhile, the people of Ireland were becoming increasingly divided along religious lines; the Great Famine affected Ulster least, and in the popular mind 'black forty-seven' was partly remembered for sectarian reasons. The wretched condition of most of the population after the famine killed political efforts for some years. The 'Young Ireland' movement attempted an uprising in 1848, but its leader, Smith O'Brien, gathered only 100 men around him. During the 1850s the government of the United Kingdom was able to concern itself less with Irish matters and concentrate instead on social legislation for industrial towns. When it had acted to legislate for Ireland it had done so in a hurry – in 1800, 1829 and 1846 – and because there was a desperate need. Other measures had preserved the existing system rather than changed it. With no threat coming out of the island, little further of consequence was done until the time of Gladstone.

Notes

(1) Government was carried out by the Lord Lieutenant (Viceroy) who was always a Peer, the Chief Secretary (always a commoner), and an Under-Secretary.

(2) The increase in Ireland's population was despite a net emigration of 1.5 million, 1815-45.

(3) O'Connell's followers in the House of Commons numbered 39 in 1832; 32 in 1835; and 31 in 1837.

(4) The tithe war of the 1830s went on unnoticed in England for much of the time because of the Reform Bills. However, in 1832, Lord Grey reported that there had been 9,000 criminal acts because of it.

Tim Chapman teaches history at Wisbech Grammar School, Cambridgeshire.

Norman Gash
Peel and Ireland: A Perennial Problem

The career of Sir Robert Peel illustrates the impact of Ireland on British politics in the first half of the nineteenth century.

Ireland shaped Peel's career more than it did that of any other nineteenth-century Prime Minister, even Gladstone. When he was a young politician, it made his reputation; in middle life it plunged him into a deep personal and public crisis; when he was at the height of his power, it produced the potato famine that precipitated the disruption of his party and the end of his leadership. No Prime Minister of the century knew so much about Ireland; few tried to do so much for Ireland; none paid so heavy a price.

Political overture

It all began accidentally. If Lord Liverpool had been successful in 1812 in his attempt to form a broad-based coalition government, he would probably have sent Lord Wellesley as Lord Lieutenant to Ireland with Huskisson as his Chief Secretary. His failure forced him to promote younger men from within his administration. One of them was Robert Peel, who has worked under him for two years as his junior under-secretary in the Department of War and Colonies. He had no previous knowledge of Ireland and he was not 25 years old. His only assets were his energy, his intellectual ability, and a zest for getting things done, though none of his predecessors since the Union of 1801 had distinguished themselves.

His six years in Ireland as Chief Secretary (1812–18) did three things for Peel. It was there that he learnt the arts of political administration. The Chief Secretary had a very varied role. He acted as a kind of prime minister in miniature to the Lord Lieutenant. He was the political channel for the latter's constitutional and legal powers, supervising all aspects of Irish government, and official spokesman for Irish administration in the House of Commons. He spent half his time in London, dealing directly with the Prime Minister and Home Secretary, having his own small office there as well as the larger office in Dublin.

Physically and mentally it was an arduous post, well-calculated to make or break the career of any aspiring politician. In the slippery world of Irish politics, Peel soon gained experience of the defects and waywardness of human nature. He had to learn how to deal with superiors and subordinates; how best to extract reliable information; how to guide policy through the obstacles of political indifference and bureaucratic inertia; how to present a convincing case in the House of Commons; when to compromise and wait; when to press forcefully ahead. In the process he developed a certain cautiousness and protective reserve of manner which remained with him for the rest of his life – not always for the good of his popularity.

The Catholic question

Like most English people new to the country, he was startled by the high level of violence and crime, which in Ireland seemed taken as normal. To a man with Peel's instinct for order and clarity, it was an intolerable state of anarchy. His first major piece of legislation was the Peace Preservation Act of 1814 which did for Ireland what the foundation of the Metropolitan Police in London was to do for England 15 years later. Under this act, Ireland was provided for the first time with a body of professional police, directed by independent salaried magistrates, ready to enforce law and order in any disturbed area of the country. It was the start of what later became the Royal Irish (and subsequently Ulster) Constabulary.

What Peel increasingly realised, however, was the complexity of social conditions which underlay the crime and disorder, in particular the economically vulnerable state of the Irish peasantry and the chaotic land system. It was this complexity that ensured, as he more than once tried to explain in the House of Commons, that there could be no quick or easy solution to Irish problems. Yet at least this widening appreciation of the deplorable economic state of the island equipped him to deal successfully with the famine of 1817, which marked the first serious failure of the potato crop since the Irish peasantry had become almost totally reliant on that one source of food. Peel's energy in extracting money for relief from a reluctant Treasury, and his efficient organisation of food distribution by local agencies in the worst-affected areas, enabled the crisis to be overcome without serious catastrophe. When he left Ireland in 1818 he had acquired, by direct administrative experience, a more comprehensive understanding of Ireland's social and economic ills than any other Englishman in public life.

In England, however, the Irish problem was largely understood in terms of Catholic emancipation. On this issue Peel's instincts were more in accord with popular English feeling. Even before he went to

Ireland he had made it clear that he sided with those who were against an immediate granting of full political equality to Roman Catholics or any settlement that did not afford full security to the established Church of England and Ireland. This was natural enough, given his orthodox Anglican and politically conservative family background. Had he held a different view, he would almost certainly not have been chosen for Ireland, since both the Prime Minister and the Lord Lieutenant were unsympathetic to Catholic claims. The government as a whole was officially neutral on the issue but, as it happened, the two most influential ministers in the Commons, Castlereagh and Canning, were both on the liberal or 'Catholic' side. In the absence of any outstanding 'Protestant' champion in the lower house, Peel found that as official representative of the Irish administration and leader of the governmental group of strongly protestant Irish MPs, it increasingly fell to him to defend that cause in public. A brilliant speech he made in 1817 materially helped to defeat Grattan's emancipation motion, earned Peel national acclaim, and won for him the coveted honour of election for Oxford University.

At the Home Office

When he resigned his Irish post in 1818 he had served three times as long as any Secretary since the Union and had acquired a reputation which made an early entry into the Cabinet almost certain. At the same time, by becoming unofficial leader of the Protestant Party in the House of Commons, when support for that cause was gradually ebbing amongst the educated classes in England, he had given a dangerous hostage to fortune. When he did get a promotion, moreover, events conspired to ensure that Ireland would remain one of his chief responsibilities. As Home Secretary 1822–27 and again 1828–30, he had general charge of Irish policy and with two inexperienced and not very strong Chief Secretaries, he felt it advisable to keep a closer watch than was usual in a Home Secretary on Irish affairs.

Administrative reform continued, notably the placing of the Irish constabulary on a national basis in 1822 and an extension of the role of the stipendiary magistrates. In the near-famine of 1823 and the equally difficult year of 1826, Peel was prompt with both advice and financial help. The most serious problem for the Irish administration in these years, however, was not economic, but political, in the shape of a renewal on a larger scale and more popular basis of the Irish agitation for Emancipation. The dissolution of the technically illegal Catholic Board in 1814 and divisions among Catholic leaders had ensured that for most of Peel's own Secretaryship the Emancipation movement in Ireland had not presented real difficulties. The foundation of the Catholic Association in 1822, however, began a new and formidable agitation which no legislation at Westminster was able to restrain. In any case the growing strength of liberal opinion in parliament put any draconian policy of repression out of question.

As early as 1825 Peel came to the conclusion that his position as the only firm Protestant advocate on the ministerial front bench in the Commons was an embarrassment both to himself and the government. He had not changed his views; he still felt that Emancipation would in the end destroy the Union; but he doubted whether resistance could be maintained much longer. In 1825 it was only the probability that his resignation would lead to that of the Prime Minister and therefore the whole government, that made him stay on. In 1827, when Lord Liverpool retired and Canning became Prime Minister, Peel was able to retire with a clear conscience; but it was only a reprieve. Less than a year later, Canning's death and the King's appeal to Wellington to form an administration put Peel back at the Home Office once more.

In 1828 his personal dilemma returned. The crisis produced by O'Connell's election for County Clare persuaded both Peel and Wellington that the only way to avoid civil strife in Ireland was to concede Emancipation. Peel's advice, conveyed to both the Prime Minister and the King, presupposed that the change of policy would be accompanied by his own resignation from office. As time passed, however, it was made increasingly plain to him by Wellington that without Peel's presence as minister in the Commons, he felt no confidence in the ability of his administration to achieve Emancipation. In the end, pressure from Wellington and the King, his own sense of loyalty – and perhaps also his own administrative instincts – made him reluctantly agree to remain in office and pilot the bill through the Commons. The cost to his political reputation was immense. He lost his seat for Oxford and raised fundamental doubts about his personal integrity and judgement. Even to neutrals it seemed that, having needlessly prolonged the resistance to Catholic claims, he had suddenly turned round and betrayed his followers. The bitter Tory and Anglican resentment, directed more against Peel than Wellington, helped to bring about the fall of the ministry the following year. It was a painful and ignominious end to the first phase of his political career.

In opposition

He was, however, still young and resilient; and the years from 1830 to 1841 proved to be a period of reconstruction for the party and restored reputation for himself. His main task in opposition was to secure unity in the shattered and divided Conservative Party and present the Whig ministry from conceding too much to their Radical and Irish allies. Irish issues still dominated much of British politics. The Anglican reaction which began the Conservative electoral revival was occasioned in fact by the government's proposals for retrenchment and reform in the Anglican Church of Ireland. Though Peel was not unsympathetic to many aspects of Whig Irish policy, he looked upon the vexed 'appropriation' issue (the question whether the property of the Church should be appropriated for secular purposes such as education) as the battle-line between the two parties. His skilful opposition tactics secured a tacit compromise by which the government dropped appropriation and the opposition accepted Whig legislation on Irish municipal corporations, tithe and poor law. By 1838 it appeared that all outstanding Irish issues had been cleared from the political agenda, leaving Peel free to concentrate on domestic matters.

Prime Minister

When the 1841 general election brought Peel to power, English affairs inevitably took precedence in his mind. There is evidence that even in the 1830s his thoughts had been moving towards a new conciliatory approach to the Irish-Catholic middle classes; but once in office, other matters took priority. The variety of problems demanding his attention – his new financial measures, the free-trade budgets, the Anti-Corn Law League agitation, Chartism, the economic distress in industrial areas, the social violence of 1842, threat of war with the USA, strained relations with France – was large enough without gratuitous additions to the list. In Ireland a policy of passivity and restraint seemed advisable. Though O'Connell, with his Whig friends out of office, at once returned to his agitation for a repeal of the Union, initially he had little success and there was no need to turn him into a political martyr. In 1843, however, the Repeal movement came explosively to life with mass meetings of peasants all over Ireland, increased financial backing, and growing support from the Catholic laity and clergy. When O'Connell overstepped the law, therefore, the government acted decisively: the 'monster' meeting at Clontarf was banned and O'Connell arrested.

The repression of disorder, however, was in Peel's mind merely the allaying of symptoms; it did nothing to cure the underlying disease. O'Connell had once more thrust Ireland into the consciousness of the British public and Peel now had the opportunity to persuade parliament of the need for more radical measures. In the autumn of 1843, a far-reaching enquiry into the relations of landlord and tenant was entrusted to a Royal Commission under Lord Devon. Reforms in this complicated and controversial field were bound to be slow; for more immediate results Peel turned to other issues. His new deal for Ireland, expounded to his colleagues in three important documents in the spring of 1844, was founded on one fundamental argument; that the Union would never be stable, and the administration of Ireland never satisfactory, until the educated Catholic community in Ireland was prepared to co-operate with the government. To obtain that, Peel was ready to make any concession short of abandoning the Union and the Church of Ireland. This courageous and radical change of policy owed everything to Peel's growing conviction that the disorder and disaffection of Ireland was a permanent cancer in the British political system, an embarrassment to its diplomacy abroad, and a potential danger in time of war. Nevertheless, the boldness of the new approach was calculated to rouse distrust and hostility both from the Protestant public in England and from Catholic nationalist sentiment in Ireland. The polarisation of Anglo-Irish relations left only a limited middle ground for a policy of concession and conciliation.

The immediate programme of legislation which Peel placed before parliament in 1844–45 had three main objects: better facilities for the private endowment of the Catholic Church in Ireland, an improvement in the training of Catholic priests, and the provision of university education in Ireland for the Catholic middle classes. He succeeded in the first two, to a greater extent (it now seems clear) than he or the British public realised at the time; he failed in the third. In view of the deep suspicions of many Irish Catholic bishops, the antagonism of Irish nationalist politicians, and the vociferous Protestant opposition in England, this was a remarkable achievement. The hardest battle came over the bill to give a generous capital grant and a greatly increased annual subvention to Maynooth College, the Catholic clerical seminary. It became law in 1845 only at the cost of splitting the Conservative Party. Of all Peel's public measures it seemed the most direct repudiation of the defence of Church and State on which the party had been rebuilt in the 1830s. Half the parliamentary party voted against it; and to more than one of Peel's cabinet colleagues it seemed that, like Catholic emancipation in 1829, Maynooth in 1845 had shattered his ascendancy as leader and would have the same ultimate consequences for his government.

Peel's Irish policy undoubtedly paved the way for the disruption of the Conservative Party in 1846, even though the repeal of the Corn Laws was an irrelevancy as far as Ireland was concerned. The Irish famine precipitated the Corn Law Crisis because the Anti-Corn Law League had made that issue the dominant one in domestic British politics. The link between the two problems was Peel's conviction that the British taxpayer could not realistically be asked to spend large sums on famine relief in Ireland while the restrictive Corn Laws remained on the statute-book in England. Free trade in corn in itself did nothing to feed the starving and penniless Irish peasants. For that the well-tried methods used by Peel in the past proved the only efficacious remedy. It was the prompt and energetic response of his government: the generous grants from the Exchequer, the purchase of food abroad, the scheme of public works to provide paid employment, the organisation of local relief committees, the direct distribution of food in the worst-hit areas, that were behind the success in dealing with the first famine year. None starved to death in Ireland while Peel remained in office.

Retrospect

Peel's handling of the famine crisis, and his conciliation policy toward Irish Catholics in 1844–45, have received full recognition from recent Irish historians. In English politics his larger programme of Irish reforms, including the main recommendations of the Devon Commission, remained as a legacy to posterity. That programme was clearly the product of a long evolution of ideas. Until 1828 his views on Ireland were doomed to sterility because the order and tranquillity which he thought might create the conditions for a prosperous and civilised community were never achieved. It is noticeable that the Home Office contribution to the government pamphlet of 1822, which must have been approved, if not actually written, by Peel, took a sombre view of the prospects of an administrative solution to Ireland's manifold ills. The change in Peel's mind came after 1829. Catholic emancipation did not, as the optimists had believed (though not Peel), bring an end to Irish agitation. It followed, in his opinion, that nothing permanent or worthwhile was likely to be achieved in Ireland until the bulk of the Catholic community were persuaded that it was in their own interest to support the administration.

From then on, his approach to the Irish problem became increasingly fertile and imaginative. Even after he had left office his mind continually turned towards that country. He thought Whig policy timid and short-sighted. The famine, he believed, and the lull in political agitation which it produced, provided an opportunity for bold initiatives of a kind that rarely occurred in Anglo-Irish relations. His last major speech on Ireland, delivered in the Commons in March 1849, was one of the most perceptive and innovative of all his commentaries on the problems of that unhappy country. He urged the government to assist in the diversification of Irish agriculture and to encourage the gradual transfer of land to the Irish peasantry. In private he let it be known that he favoured direct endowment of the Irish Catholic clergy. His ideas on how to put right the defective social and economic structure of Ireland were a generation ahead of their time; but they anticipated nearly all the reforms which subsequent British governments up to 1914 belatedly tried to carry out. After Peel it was not ideas on Ireland that were lacking, only the political will and capability.

There was, however, another, more pessimistic, but no less realistic lesson to be drawn from Peel's career: the immense gulf of prejudice and history which separated the fundamental attitudes of English and Irish national politicians; the suspicion on both sides likely to be encountered by any British statesman who tried to bridge that gulf; and political perils to himself if he persisted too far.

Further Reading

Dudley Edwards, R. and Williams, T. D. (eds) *The Great Famine* (Browne and Nolan, 1956).

Gash, N. *Mr Secretary Peel* (Longman, 1961).

Gash, N. *Sir Robert Peel* (Longman, 1972).

Gash, N. *Peel* (Longman, 1976).

Kerr, D. A. *Peel, Priests and Politics* (Oxford University Press, 1982).

O'Tuathaigh, G. *Ireland Before the Famine 1789–1846*, vol. 9 of the Gill and *History of Ireland* (Gill and Macmillan, 1972).

Machin, A. *The Catholic Question in English Politics 1820–30* (Clarendon Press, 1964).

Norman Gash is Emeritus Professor of History at the University of St. Andrews.

Ruscombe Foster
Peel and his Party:
The 'Age of Peel' Reassessed

Why did the Conservative Party turn against Peel in 1846? It is argued here that Peel's political dominance was much less secure than some have claimed, and the party's objections to his policy are explored.

Sir Robert Peel was Prime Minister of a majority Conservative government for only five years in an era dominated by Whig governments, and yet it has become almost axiomatic to view the generation after 1832 as the 'Age of Peel'. The paradox has two explanations. First, there is the undoubted fact that whether in government or opposition Peel dominated the House of Commons for the last 20 years of his life. Second, there are the historical labours of Professor Norman Gash. According to Gash, Peel was the man who imparted the old and seemingly reactionary Tory Party of 1832 with the new and progressive image of Conservatism. The result was sensational, for within a decade of their electoral nadir at the election of December 1832 they were to win a spectacular victory. Once in office, Peel set about putting his Conservative theory into practice. The economy was righted, though only at the cost of splitting the party and bringing an abrupt end to his Premiership, following the decision to repeal the corn laws in 1846. Typically on this occasion, Peel had put what he saw as national above mere party interests. His premature death in 1850 as the result of a riding accident completed his martyrdom. Hindsight, moreover, seemed to vindicate his actions, for whilst the economy flourished for a generation, the backward-looking Protectionist rump, shorn of its Peelite talent, had to relearn slowly the lessons which the master had taught them. As Gash puts it: 'His place as the founder of modern Conservatism is unchallengable ... The age of revolt was giving way to the age of stability; and of that age Peel had been the chief architect.' Recent work, however, suggests that Peel's reputation is based less on historiography than hagiography.

Leader of the Conservative Party?

Peel's domination of the lower chamber was admitted even by his opponents. Disraeli commented famously that Peel would 'play upon the House of Commons like an old fiddle'. His influence there made it essential for Wellington to retain Peel in his government when

Catholic Emancipation Reform was introduced in 1829. During the Reform Bill debates, Peel's speeches were the most polished and intellectual expositions of the anti-reformers' case. They impressed moderate Reformers such as Sir George Staunton, who confidently predicted in his diary that Peel would be the central figure in the Commons once the Reform issue was settled. Peel could be memorably witty too, as when in 1840 he ridiculed the hapless Sir Francis Baring: 'Can there be a more lamentable picture than that of a Chancellor of the Exchequer seated on an empty chest – by the pool of a bottomless deficiency – fishing for a budget.' As Prime Minister the mastery was complete, for he seemed to have the detail of every department at his fingertips, making him, in Gladstone's opinion, 'the best man of business who was ever Prime Minister'.

To say that Peel dominated the House of Commons, however, is not the same as saying that he dominated Parliament, or even his own party in Parliament. It is too easily forgotten that many other political giants of the day – Liverpool, Wellington, Derby, Aberdeen, Grey, Brougham and Melbourne – all sat in the House of Lords, and that many of the great debates took place there. Amongst the great Tory majority in the Upper House, particularly within the ranks of the Ultras, there existed little respect or affection for Peel. Regarded by them as the villain of the piece for his switch of loyalties in 1829, he was thereafter always viewed with suspicion and mistrust. During the passage of the Municipal Corporations Act in 1835, Lord Lyndhurst is supposed to have thundered 'Damn Peel. What is Peel to me? Damn him!' when Peel wanted the Tory peers to endorse his amendments rather than wreck the measure. Though he led the party in the Commons therefore, Peel's obstacles to leading the party as a whole might have been insurmountable were it not for the assistance rendered him by the Duke of Wellington in the Lords.

Wellington alone possessed the prestige necessary to cajole, persuade or threaten recalcitrant peers who might otherwise have pursued an independent course of action. Certainly during the 1830s, one should think in terms of a genuinely dual leadership of the Conservative Party. After all, it was Wellington who had been Tory Prime Minister between 1828 and 1830, Wellington who was asked to form an administration during the 'May Days' of 1832 and Wellington who was sent for in November 1834 when the Whig government was dismissed. It was only at Wellington's insistence that Peel was then made Prime Minister. Even this experience of the first office, however, did not absolutely confirm Peel's position. It was to Wellington that Melbourne made overtures for a possible coalition during the later 1830s and Wellington who was summoned during the Bedchamber crisis of 1839. Contemporaries certainly regarded this idea of dual leadership as more or less fact. Sir James Graham, subsequently to become the most dedicated of all Peel's disciples, wrote candidly to the Duke in the mid-1830s that he regarded them both as leader. Even after 1841 a strong popular notion persisted that Wellington, Minister without Portfolio in the cabinet, remained a guiding force on policy. He was regularly portrayed in cartoons either behind Peel or as his indispensable drill sergeant. Perhaps the notion is not without substance. Neville Thompson, Wellington's latest biographer, is convinced that only Wellington could have secured the passage of the Maynooth Grant through the House of Lords in 1845 and smoothed that of corn law repeal in 1846. If the age is to be epitomised in the names of Conservative statesmen, then it must surely be of Wellington and Peel together.

The road to 1841

The *Quarterly Review* hailed the Conservative election victory of 1841 as a personal triumph for Peel. Many modern historians have agreed in seeing Peel's contribution as the decisive one. The gospel of cautious progressivism as preached in the Tamworth Manifesto of December 1834 had apparently carried the day in converting or reconverting the political middle ground to the Conservative cause. Plenty of ex-party evidence can be adduced to support this interpretation. William Sturges-Bourne, for example, Home Secretary in Canning's shortlived ministry in 1827, re-entered active politics in 1834 on the strength of Peel's moderation. Conservative candidates in many constituencies – even Disraeli in 1835 – had pledged their general allegiance to the principles of Tamworth.

Whilst one would not seek to gainsay that Peel made a contribution to the triumph of 1841, one must now call into doubt whether it was decisive. In the first place it is easy to exaggerate the uniqueness of what he said in the Tamworth Manifesto. The oft-quoted phrases, for example pledging a 'careful review of institutions, both civil and ecclesiastical' and 'the correction of proved abuses and the redress of real grievances' are remarkably similar to most Whig election addresses of the period. The following is an extract from the address of a member of the Whig government at the 1835 election:

Reform I deem that which strengthens, purifies, and exalts the constitutional establishment of the country, and not that which is calculated by a blind and furious zeal for innovation, to impair, degrade and destroy its venerated institutions.

Seen in this context, Peelite Conservatism seems more like an echo than a voice. In judging between these two variations on the same theme, floating voters were probably less influenced by what the competing parties said than by the fact that by the late 1830s a lacklustre Whig government was becoming increasingly dependent upon Radical and Irish support for its survival. It was thus more likely to capitulate to demands for extensive and unpalatable reforms. The government also had to carry the blame for unpopular measures such as the 1834 Poor Law Amendment Act and the downturn in the economy. All these factors contributed to its demise without Peel having to say or do anything.

It is also important to appreciate that whilst some Conservatives were happy to endorse Peel's sentiments, others were wary of them and correspondingly cautious to avoid giving him pledges of unconditional support. In English county constituencies, Conservative candidates were more inclined to emphasise their attachment to crown, church and aristocracy, those traditional rallying cries of the old Tory Party before 1832. As the 1841 election approached and as the activities of the Anti-Corn Law League increased, they added the immutability of the corn laws to their banner. John Fleming, Conservative MP for South Hampshire from 1835 onwards, boasted at an election dinner in 1840 that he had opposed every major reform of the previous decade. His subsequent unopposed return was hardly a triumph for Peelite Conservatism.

Such statistical evidence as is available suggests that it was the uncompromising old-style Toryism, exemplified by Fleming, which attracted most support and thus does most to explain the Conservative revival up to 1841. In 1832 the party won only 42 of the 144 English county seats, but by 1841 they had recovered enough to secure 124 seats in what was, after all, their traditional heartland. The party also polled comparatively well in the smaller English boroughs, usually market towns, which shared the same political outlook as the surrounding countryside. Peel had therefore failed in his efforts to mould the party in his own image. Were it needed, the events of 1845–46 provided final proof of that fact.

The fear factor

Irrespective of whether one approved of Peel's actions, it has been customary to praise him for his altruism and for having had the courage of his convictions once in office. For some, however, the crisis of 1845–46 seemed to confirm the lingering doubt that Peel essentially lacked resolution in defence of Conservative interests, that he was more inclined to capitulate than to face out popular pressure. The seeds of this doubt were sown in 1829. Peel's conversion to Catholic emancipation is generally accepted to have been based on the conviction that civil war in Ireland was the unacceptable alternative, not on the merits of emancipation itself. The more combative Wellington, who also resented Peel's failure to stand by him in November 1830 and May 1832, told Lady Salisbury in 1833 that Peel's whole political strategy was ' ... nothing but weakness... He is afraid ... afraid of everything.' For Wellington therefore, the Corn Law crisis was a case of *déjà vu*, for Peel seemed again to be capitulating in face of the spectre of civil unrest in Ireland which loomed as a result of the potato famine. 'Rotten potatoes have done it all', he fumed. 'They put Peel in his damned fright.' This famous outburst is usually dismissed as an old man's irascibility. Perhaps it should be taken more seriously. After all, it was accepted that repeal could not immediately alleviate the plight of the Irish peasant and it is a moot point amongst academics as to whether the Corn Laws in reality hamstrung the British economy. It looks more plausible that Peel was galvanised into action (using the Irish situation as a pretext) through fear that if he did not act, the Anti-Corn Law League would use the disaster to increase social unrest on the free trade issue in England. His infamous encomium on Cobden as the man responsible for repeal, in a speech which was deeply resented in many official Tory circles, may well therefore have been meant literally, for it was only owing to the League that the corn laws had become so emotive.

A fear of mob disorder, therefore, may have played a bigger part in Peel's decision making than he would readily admit. But such fears undoubtedly existed, for as Professor Evans has recently pointed out, Peel was to fortify his home against possible attack more times than any Prime Minister of the nineteenth century.

Peel and the party system

Whatever his *leitmotif*, Peel wanted to conserve the aristocratic constitution as much as any Ultra, but Conservatives differed as to how this was to be achieved. Peel believed that the nation's economic ills lay at the root of the social tension which threatened the hierarchical status quo. Thus financial policy, inspired by his *laissez-faire* ideology, took top priority once he was in office. In putting his policies into effect, Peel demanded that the Parliamentary Party accept his diagnosis of what was best for the country without question. This approach was highlighted during the 1844 session when Peel twice threatened resignation over the issues of sugar duties and the hours of factory labour, and succeeded in getting the Commons to reverse earlier votes on the matters. Backbenchers faced with such ultimatums preferred to toe the line rather than risk the return of a Whig government.

Seeing these events through Peel's eyes, his biographers have been sympathetic to his conduct. In fact Peel's actions reveal a poor appreciation of the ordinary backbencher's position. By his own admission, a man with little time for the all-important communication between leaders and led, he held the party rank and file in near contempt. He complained to his wife in 1845:

> How can those who spend their time hunting and shooting and eating and drinking know what were the motives of those who are responsible for the public security, who have access to the best information, and have no other object under heaven but to provide against danger and consult the general interests of all classes.

These comments betray a cool arrogance and sense of a superior intellect, but they amount to a poor caricature. The sort of person included in Peel's tirade was Sir William Heathcote, a man respected on all sides of the House and one who took his duties in local government, as a county MP and as a paternal landlord with exemplary seriousness. His intellectual prowess subsequently won him the invitation to sit with Gladstone as one of the Members for Oxford University and Disraeli identified him as possessed of the ideal qualities to be found in a country gentleman worthy to lead the Protectionist Party in Parliament. Heathcote came to oppose Peel, not through the gut reactions of a blinkered backwoodsman, but because intellect allied to constituency pressure convinced him that Peel was betraying vital Conservative interests. Peel, it might be remembered, had never sat for anything that could be remotely described as a popular constituency.

Underpinning Peel's particular disregard of his own backbenchers was his poor appreciation of the changing nature of the party political system after 1832. Governments before 1832, by means of patronage and the disinclination of independents to remove the king's ministers, could usually rely on the House of Commons to endorse its chosen course of action. As the amount of patronage available declined, and as politics became more polarised, this ceased to be the case. Party came to be the indispensable support of a government and in return expected that its general interests be taken care of. Though he was aware of the change, Peel never properly accommodated himself to it. He was content for the party to sustain him in office, but he made no secret of the fact that he would not allow it in any way to dictate policy: Peel alone would judge what measures constituted the national interest. This amounted to an unrealistically one-sided relationship which might – and did – not last for ever. It is worth remembering that Disraeli's charge against Peel in 1846 was not that he was abandoning protection, but that he was not playing the party game according to the new rules which were being evolved. As he put it:

... if you are to have a popular government – if you are to have a Parliamentary Administration – the conditions antecedent are that you should have a government which declares the principles upon which its policy is founded and then you can have the wholesome check of a constitutional Opposition. What have we got instead? ... we have a great Parliamentary middleman. It is well known what a middleman is; he is a man who bamboozles one party and plunders the other, till, having obtained a position to which he is not entitled, he cries out 'Let us have no party questions, but fixity of tenure'.

Accepting this analysis, Peel had unquestionably betrayed the party; it treated him accordingly.

Conclusion

Peel of course reasoned differently. In his view he had performed the landed interest a signal service in removing a major source of resentment against it. His pique, and his subsequent refusal to dirty his hands further in the world of party politics after 1846, is readily comprehensible. But in adopting such a lofty approach it was he and his followers who were the losers, for without a party they lacked the means to executive office for which their talents undeniably fitted them. As even Gladstone was later to admit, Peel's position for the last four years of his life was 'thoroughly false.' For all that the death of their leader in 1850 came as a personal tragedy, politically it must have been greeted by some of the Peelites almost with relief.

Further Reading

Adelman, P. *Peel and the Conservative Party 1830–50* (Longman, 1989).
Blake, R. *The Conservative Party from Peel to Thatcher* (Fontana, 1985).
Coleman, B. *Conservatism and the Conservative Party in Nineteenth-Century Britain* (Edward Arnold, 1988).
Evans, E. *Sir Robert Peel* (Routledge, 1991).
Gash, N. *Sir Robert Peel* (Longman, 1972).
Read, D. *Peel and the Victorians* (Basil Blackwell, 1987).

Ruscombe Foster is Head of History and Politics at Embley Park School, Romsey in Hampshire.

PART III
Liberals and Conservatives in Mid-Century Britain

The split in the Conservative Party after 1846 was followed by a period of political instability. Thereafter the Conservatives, shorn of their Peelite elements, could not achieve a majority. The Whig-led coalition that succeeded Peel in office was electorally dominant, but internally divided. This was still, despite the effects of the 1832 Reform Act, a period of fluid party loyalties and alliances in Parliament and the country. It was only after the various Whig-led groups had come together with the Peelites in 1859, that stability began to return. By then the Conservatives had dropped the idea of restoring agricultural protection. Gladstone, meanwhile, pressed ahead with completing free trade, dropping all duties except those for revenue purposes in 1860–61, and reducing the income tax Peel had reintroduced in 1842.

There were also other reforms; such as divorce reform in 1857, a series of legal and penal reforms and the removal in 1858 of barriers to Jews entering Parliament and of property qualifications for MPs. There were also efforts to improve the state by administrative, as well as constitutional, reform. The fall of Aberdeen's government in 1855 and his replacement by an unenthusiastic Palmerston meant that the administrative reform movement achieved little at the time. There were, however, alongside Gladstone's efforts to reduce the tax burden of the state, a series of measures to improve the scrutiny of public expenditure. These included the establishment of the Public Accounts Committee of the Commons in 1861 and the creation of the office of Comptroller and Auditor General in 1866. The spread of government intervention into new fields during the first half of the nineteenth century had seen a steady rise in public expenditure and the number of civil servants, pointing to the need for new financial controls. Meanwhile, a concern to contain and reduce the extravagance of 'Old Corruption' remained a characteristic of mid-Victorian politics. Radicals, such as the Reform Union in the 1868 general election, continued to urge the need to reduce this enormous expenditure and resulting taxation.

Norman Gash
The Peelites after Peel

The political instability that followed the fall of Peel ended when the remnants of the Peelites joined Palmerston's government in 1859.

It is sometimes argued that the chief reason for the instability of mid-Victorian party politics was the presence of the Peelites as a parliamentary group floating between the two main political parties. It would probably be more accurate to regard them as being only one of a number of causes of that instability. The emergence of an organised two-party system in the 1830s had been a consequence of the abnormal tensions of the constitutional crisis of 1828–32. It was a precocious growth which did not have deep enough roots in the constituencies to maintain its early vigour. Over the longer period, from the first to the second Reform Act, the smallness of the electorate, the survival of pre-reform electoral habits, and the absence of effective sanctions against rebellious party members, made this the last golden age of the independent MP. It was difficult for either of the two larger parties to secure working majorities in the House of Commons. The Whig-Liberal Party was weakened by the uncertain allegiance of its Radical and Irish elements, and by the personal rivalry between Lord John Russell and Palmerston. As for the Conservatives, not only had they been disrupted by the Repeal of the Corn Laws but many who followed Lord Stanley were unwilling to accept Disraeli as their leader in the lower house. It is significant that the only successful parliamentary politician of the 1850–65 period – Palmerston – was a man able to attract support from both sides of the Commons.

Peelite principles and attitudes

While Peel was alive, there was always hope for his followers that sooner or later he would return to power, even though Peel had refused to organise a Peelite 'party' and seemed content to keep the Whigs in office. After his death, however, there was no realistic prospect that his ex-colleagues could ever form a ministry by themselves or even continue long as a separate political group. Their dilemma therefore was to decide with which political party they should throw in their lot and when that step should be taken. It was not a crude question of seizing the first opportunity to resume their individual ministerial careers. They felt that they represented certain important principles in public life: the safeguarding of Peel's achievements, the pursuit of fiscal correctness and administrative rectitude, the maintenance of a peaceful foreign policy, and the exercise of a tolerant liberalism in religious matters. Though they did not claim that these high-minded ideals were peculiar to themselves, they did not think that either of the two larger parties had a satisfactory record in these respects.

In particular, the Peelites distrusted on the one side the basic protectionist instincts of the party of Lord Stanley (soon to be Lord Derby in 1851) and the aggressive Protestantism which lurked in its ranks; on the other side, Palmerston's reckless diplomacy, the nepotism and incompetence of the Whig oligarchy, and Russell's tendency to put forward further schemes of parliamentary reform. Underneath these public attitudes were more personal feelings. Many of them saw Palmerston as an opportunistic careerist with few convictions, at any rate in domestic matters; and Russell as an inept and erratic politician for whom it was difficult to have any respect. Many also bore lasting resentment at the unscrupulous personal attacks on Peel by the Protectionists during the Corn Law debates of 1846 and despised Disraeli as an unprincipled adventurer. This was particularly true of Gladstone. Although of all the leading Peelites he felt perhaps least loyalty to Peel's memory and remained on cordial terms with Lord Derby, he had an unconquerable aversion to his lieutenant in the Commons. The hard inner truth was that if Gladstone rejoined the main body of Conservatives, he would either have to displace Disraeli or reconcile himself to serving under him.

Gladstone is an illustration in one man of the perplexities of the Peelites as a whole. He was by common consent the ablest of the Peelites and their natural leader in the lower house. As a Conservative and a High Churchman he hankered intellectually for a reunion with the rump of the old Conservative Party, while year by year his personal emotions, his liberal sympathies and his political ambitions were carrying him in an opposite direction. It is not surprising, therefore, that none of the prominent Peelites felt able to give a forceful lead in guiding his colleagues towards one or other of the two main parties. If Gladstone was not in a position to do so, it was unlikely that any of the other younger men would take the task on himself; and the older Peelites, Aberdeen and Graham, had few political ambitions left.

Nature of the Peelite party

Moreover, there was always a doubt about the readiness of their nominal followers to follow them in any such decisive move. The existence of a Peelite party was generally accepted by the politicians, the newspapers and the public. Nevertheless, to define it was a puzzle which defied expert commentators at the time and historians ever since. To draw up accurate lists of its adherents was difficult; to predict their voting behaviour was a matter of guess work. They fell into no easily recognisable category. As far as the social background and type of constituency were concerned, there was nothing to distinguish Peelite Conservatives from the mass of the old united Conservative Party. The only way of identifying them was by their public declarations and their actions in the House of Commons; and these were often too inconsistent to be reliable criteria.

To name the Peelites' leaders was easy enough. They consisted of Peel's former ministerial colleagues who stood by him in 1846 and remained active and independent in parliamentary politics after 1850: Aberdeen and Graham of the older generation, and about half a dozen younger men headed by Gladstone. Around this nucleus was a larger number of backbench MPs who followed the general Peelite line and were assumed to be ready to support any administration which they could recognise as formed on Peelite principles and containing a number of his old ministers. Further removed from the centre was a loose array of men who variously described themselves as Liberal or Free Trade or Independent Conservatives. They could be relied on to vote against any attempt to restore the Corn Laws; but when other issues came up in Parliament – foreign policy, religion, financial relief to agriculture, or the maintenance in office of a Whig ministry – there were divided views, divided interests and divided voting, in which constituency pressures as well as personal convictions played a large part.

As time passed, the Peelite numbers in the Commons steadily dwindled. Men died or retired, were beaten in elections, or quietly changed their minds and slipped into the shelter of the main Liberal or Conservative Parties as a more comfortable way of continuing their parliamentary careers. It was to these miscellaneous causes, rather than to any dramatic 'defeat' at a general election, that the numerical decline of the Peelites is to be attributed. To some extent this was offset by the arrival in the Commons of new members who identified themselves as Peelites; but they were only enough to slow down, never to halt, the inexorable process of attrition. In very broad terms (and it is misleading to present estimates of Peelite strength except in this way) the general body of Peelites after the general election of 1847 numbered between 70 and 80. In the post-1852 House of Commons there were between 40 and 50. But these figures can easily be moved up or down, depending on the stringency of the classification employed.

Peelite tactics

In these circumstances it is easy to see why there was a standing temptation for senior Peelites to fall back on the attitude of waiting to see how events shaped before committing themselves to any action. In 1851, this policy of opportunism had much to recommend it. Yet in the long run it had considerable drawbacks, not least of which was the reputation for aloofness and inconsistency which it created. Though, in retrospect, it may seem obvious that the general drift was towards a junction with the Whig-Liberal Party, there were many cross-currents which bore them off course.

At heart the Peelites felt themselves to be Conservatives. It was not easy for them to shake off that identity. The Whigs had been their historical opponents and the Peelites were sensitive to the thought that if they now went over to their side, they would be taunted with having changed their colours, merely for the sake of office. Even Sir James Graham, the ex-Whig converted to Peelite Conservatism in 1835–37, who showed increasing cordiality towards Russell after 1850, was unwilling to return to the party of his political youth, if it meant that he would have to make that journey alone. For the younger Peelites such as Gladstone, who had been hand-picked for office by Peel, it was hard to accept that only the Whig-Liberal Party offered the prospect of resuming their interrupted ministerial careers. In fact Gladstone, Herbert and Cardwell retained their membership of the Conservative Carlton Club until 1859.

The Peelites were aware, of course, that they constituted a pool of talent and experience which would be invaluable to either of the two larger parties. In the middle decades of the century both Liberals and Conservatives, for different reasons, were conspicuously deficient in men of ministerial quality. Russell, Derby and Palmerston all in turn made repeated offers to particular Peelites and even when rebuffed, continued to cultivate good relations with them generally. But there were difficulties here, too. To recruit individual Peelites for high office was an obvious tactic for a leader conscious of his own party's shortcomings. To secure a complete fusion with the whole body of Peelites was a more difficult operation. Large parties do not take kindly to accommodating former opponents. The difficulties, however, were not all on one side. Neither of these two possibilities were particularly agreeable to the Peelite leaders themselves. They wished to stay together, rather than be picked off one by one; and if it was a question of a junction of parties, they wanted it to be an alliance of equals, rather than a merger in which their small party would be extinguished by the larger body. To a strong sense of their own political value, they added an equally strong sense of unity based on personal friendship. This was especially true of the younger group of Peelites – Gladstone, Lincoln (who became Duke of Newcastle in 1851), Sidney Herbert, Dalhousie, Canning and Cardwell. They were much the same age; and all of them were Oxford men, five from the same college, Christ Church. None of the leading Peelites wished to break up this solidarity, however exasperating it was for politicians in other parties.

The Aberdeen coalition

The ambiguities of the Peelite position were seen as early as 1851, when Russell resigned. Aberdeen and Graham refused to meet the queen's desire for a Whig-Peelite coalition; and when Stanley agreed to attempt a ministry, Aberdeen discouraged Gladstone from accepting his invitation to serve in it. There were in fact good reasons for the Peelites to hold off from both main parties at that juncture. Russell's recent anti-papal legislation and his renewed interest in a further measure of parliamentary reform were equally distasteful to the Peelite concept of moderate, progressive liberalism. There was also a feeling that Stanley should be allowed an opportunity to form a protectionist government, if only to demonstrate that it would be doomed to failure. By the following year the political scene had taken on a firmer shape. The quarrel between Russell and Palmerston had brought about the collapse of the Whig administration in a more emphatic manner than the temporary resignation of 1851. On the other hand, the general election of 1852 had not only failed to give Derby a majority in the Commons, but had soiled his party's reputation by its electoral scandals and the inability of Conservative candidates in different constituencies to speak with one voice on the issue of protection. The Peelites therefore were able to appear as saviours of the political constitution.

The Aberdeen coalition was thus a natural and logical solution for a crisis created by the damaged fortunes and damaged reputations of the two major parties. Indeed, after Gladstone's almost single-handed destruction of Disraeli's budget, it would have been morally impossible for the Peelites to have shirked the responsibilities of office. It was the highpoint of Peelite influence in the post-1850 period. Their most senior and respected figure became Prime Minister and they secured nearly half the cabinet posts. It was a handsome reward for entering into a coalition with the Whigs: too handsome, in the view of some Whigs.

Yet it would be difficult to argue that the Whigs paid too high a price for the Aberdeen coalition. It was their own weaknesses and divisions over a long period which brought on the crisis; and no Whig politician of any outstanding merit had been passed over for office. Though it was patently true that the Peelites could only bring a relatively small number of votes into the government lobby, there were other equally important ways in which they helped cement the parliamentary strength of the new administration. Their presence in the government was influential in conciliating both the Irish Catholic MPs disgruntled by Russell's anti-papal legislation and the doctrinaire free-trade Radicals who doubted the commitment of the great Whig landowners to a firm anti-protectionist policy. It was probably reassuring too for many independent Conservatives on the opposition benches, of whom a sizeable number regularly voted with Aberdeen's government.

Ironically it was the prominent position of the Peelites in the ministry which made the Crimean War so disastrous to them personally. The public outcry over the early disasters of the campaign destroyed Aberdeen's career and led eventually to the collective Peelite resignation from Palmerston's administration in 1855. It was bad luck for the Peelites, whose reputation was based on domestic achievements, that their first experiment of participating in a Liberal coalition was wrecked by an unexpected and unnecessary war. What made it so damaging was that three of their number – Aberdeen as Prime Minister, Newcastle at the War Office and Graham at the Admiralty – bore direct personal responsibility for the actual conduct of hostilities. The Crimean 'disasters' were less serious than they were made to appear at the time; and owed more to the strategic folly of the war itself and the long financial neglect of the armed forces since 1815 than to any mistakes by individual ministers at the time.

From the point of view of party development, however, the Aberdeen coalition had another significance. Though the Peelites entered the coalition as a group and left it as a group, while in office they had acted as loyal members of a collective administration and the divisions in the cabinet had never been on party lines. To that extent the way had been cleared for a permanent junction with the Whigs when circumstances once more made that possible. In fact no Peelite who took office in the Aberdeen coalition ever subsequently joined a Conservative administration.

The final phase

Yet, although Aberdeen and Herbert came to believe that the 1852 coalition had been the crucial event which decided the destiny of the Peelites, this was by no means obvious at the time. The high moral ground which the Peelites affected (to the annoyance of other more mundane politicians) had been shaken and their prestige tarnished. They themselves were sore at their treatment by both Russell and Palmerston, and were in no mood for early reconciliation. In the winter of 1856–57, Lord Derby expressed an anxiety to coordinate tactics in the Commons between his followers and the Peelites against Palmerston's financial policy: and Peelites joined the motley collection of Conservatives, Radicals and Liberals which brought down Palmerston on the fortuitous but emotive Chinese issue in March 1857. Derby even tried to secure an electoral pact with the Peelites in the general election which followed. The political truth that emerged from these events, however, was that the Peelites as a body had neither unity nor consistency in their attitude towards the veteran and popular Palmerston. After the election of 1857 it was accepted by the political press and by the Peelite leaders themselves that as a 'party' they had ceased to exist. There were still some three dozen MPs remaining of the original 112 Conservatives who had voted with Peel on the second reading of the repeal of the Corn Laws in 1846; but most of them had either joined, or had made up their mind to join, one or other of the two main parties. The tiny group of Peelite leaders in the Commons were officers without an army. Their consciousness of this was a powerful factor in leading them to a decision on their own future.

Herbert and Cardwell, who by now regarded themselves as committed Liberals, played an important part in opposing Derby's brief 1858 minority administration (in which both Gladstone and Newcastle refused invitations to serve) and were active in the internal talks on Liberal unity that paved the way for Palmerston's assumption of party leadership. Both men, together with Newcastle and Gladstone, were given office in the new Liberal government of 1859. It was not a difficult decision for them to make; not even for Gladstone, who up to the last had quixotically cast his vote in the Commons in support of Derby's ministry. It was clear that the country was tired of party divisions, and that Palmerston was the only national leader capable of forming a strong administration. In domestic affairs he was as conservative as any Tory; and on the main foreign policy issue of Italian unification, Gladstone for once agreed with him.

The junction of the Peelites with Palmerston in 1859 was the final event which had decided that the Peelite legacy would be passed on to the Victorian Liberal Party, rather than to the Conservative Party of Derby and Disraeli. Though the more probable, it was not the inevitable outcome of the tortuous course of politics since 1850. Had Lord Derby been ruthless enough in 1851–52 to repudiate Protectionism and sacrifice Disraeli, things might have been different. As it turned out, 1859 simply confirmed the provisional decision embodied in the unlucky Aberdeen coalition of 1852.

Further Reading

Conacher, J. B. *The Aberdeen Coalition 1852–55* (Cambridge University Press, 1968).

Conacher, J. B. *The Peelites and the Party System 1846–52* (David and Charles, 1972).

Jones, W. D. and Erickson, A. B. *The Peelites* (Ohio State University Press, 1972).

Southgate, D. *The Passing of the Whigs 1832–86* (Macmillan, 1962).

Norman Gash is Emeritus Professor of History at the University of St Andrews.

John Vincent
John the Baptist of Gladstonian Liberalism

Social and religious conflicts in which John Bright, not least in his work for the Anti-Corn Law League, played a most important part, were key features of nineteenth century politics.

Back in 1960, my venerable research supervisor, Dr Kitson Clark, talked of his family memories of John Bright, once a guest at his home. His mother, then a girl, had taken the great man his morning cup of tea. Peering out at the thick Leeds fog, she ventured to say, 'Not a very good morning, Mr Bright!' From beneath the bedclothes came the rebuke, 'Young woman, every morning that the Lord chooses to send is a *good* morning.'

For John Bright was born and bred a disapprover. As a Quaker, he grew up disapproving of art, of music, of the theatre, of alcoholic drinks, of Shakespeare. He kept no wine in the house. In public life, too, he was always *against* something: against the Corn Laws, against the Crimean War, against aristocratic government, against the Church of England and its oppressions, and against American slavery. What he was for, was not quite so clear. His oratory, inside and outside parliament, reflected Victorian values – earnestness, passion, moral indignation, sentiment – rather than a carefully worked out political programme. In public as in private, he was the last great puritan.

John Bright was important in four ways. He represented the point at which the losers in the English Civil War at last, after two centuries in the wilderness, rejoined the victors – the Anglican aristocracy – in the mainstream of public life. In this respect he was a healer. Secondly, he stood for a less exclusive England, and thus in Victorian Liberal terms, a better England. He became a cabinet minister, and more important a national symbol, without having the slightest connection with the landed gentry, without belonging to the Church of England, and without having a country mansion or estate. Indeed, he was a figure of national importance well before entering the first Gladstone cabinet in 1868.

Thirdly, he was the greatest orator of his age. He had a clear bell-like voice. He did not have Gladstone's northern accent. His language was drawn from the Bible and Milton. He was simple, where Gladstone was complex; moving, where Disraeli was only clever. His speeches touched the heart of the common man, yet were long read and studied as a contribution to serious literature. His appeals to the people marked out the path that Gladstone, with his greater advantages and abilities, was soon to follow.

Fourthly, and paradoxically, he perhaps strengthened the old aristocratic system he so disliked. Needless to say, he did not intend this. But in the 1840s the Anti-Corn Law League did much to change the nature of the Conservative Party, from a Peelite centre party with some progressive aspects, to a Derbyite, reactionary, exclusive gentry party. In 1855–65, the decade dominated by Lord Palmerston's reactionary Liberalism, the threat of Bright's supposed wish to make Britain like America was often used to make the ruling class close ranks. And Bright's membership of Gladstone's cabinets in 1868–70, 1873–74, and 1880–82, lent apparently sound radical credentials to governments which were still dominated by aristocratic administrators of traditional cultural background. Bright's radical reputation was used as camouflage, by Gladstone in particular, screening the leisurely modification of the old order.

John Bright as a Dissenter

Bright was the greatest Dissenter in public life since Cromwell. His whole character was formed by a religious tradition very different from that of the Church of England. He was heir to Milton and John Bunyan. Milton, he said, was 'the greatest man who had ever lived'. This legacy from the seventeenth century was a living thing to him.

A forebear had been imprisoned for his religious beliefs. 'I knew,' Bright recalled of his youth, 'that I came of the stock of martyrs.' His father had his belongings seized more than 20 times between 1811 and 1833 for refusing to pay church rates to a Church of England in which he did not believe. 'I don't like the Church', John Bright would say, 'so long as it steals silver spoons.' Though by his social position an employer, a master, a leader in local affairs, Bright grew up knowing what it was to be an underdog.

John Bright's early life was dominated by Quakerism, at a time when Quakers married only Quakers, and were expelled if they married outside their sect. He went, between the ages of 10 and 15, to four small Quaker boarding schools, one coeducational, in the northern counties. As was normal for a middle-class boy, Bright left school at 15, whereas a gentleman's son would have stayed until 18.

At 15, he began work in the mill office. His real education took place only after he left school. Rising at 5.30 to unlock the mill, he studied undisturbed in his cubby-hole near the boiler until breakfast. He had no guide or teacher other than the great books revered by all protestants. The Quakers of his day were religious, not political. Indeed, they thought politics a danger to the soul.

Bright's rejection of his background

The first Quaker MP was elected in 1832. Bright might have followed in his footsteps, as spokesman for a religious minority, instead of becoming as he did the leader of a broad popular Radicalism. Bright was in fact an odd man out among the Quakers, as well as among Dissenters generally. Thus he early gave up the distinctive Quaker garb in favour of modern clothes, though *Punch* continued, quite wrongly, to portray him as wearing the antique Quaker costume. The Quakers were a small, old-fashioned sect in rapid decline in his day, with not much in common with the far more numerous, combative and swiftly growing Congregationalists, Baptists, and Presbyterians, the proud heirs of those who had lost in the religious settlement of 1662. Nor did Bright share the still half-Anglican attitudes of the great Wesleyan Methodist body, not to be a Church in its own right until 1872. Dissent, for most of Bright's long career, was a mixture of separate sects, not yet conjoined in the 'Nonconformist conscience' of the Free Churches of the late Victorian era.

Had he not been a Quaker, it was said, Bright would have been a prize-fighter. He was instinctively pugnacious. In his view, anyone who opposed his principles was a 'fool or a knave', in his favourite phrase. He was not quite an ordinary pacifist, for all his love of peace. Where Quakers opposed war, he opposed aristocratic war, which was not quite the same thing. In the American Civil War, he sought a Northern victory, not a cessation of bloodshed – a conventionally progressive, rather than Quaker, attitude. And at home, and in the Quaker meeting, he rarely spoke of religion.

John Bright was thus many things at once. He represented, with some reservations, one of the two great English religious traditions. He also represented business and businessmen – those whom the Lancashire gentry despised as 'cottontots' and 'spinners of coarse yarns', as they crudely put it. But besides representing business – and he was certainly a militant capitalist and opponent of trade unions – he was also the champion of the poor. In this few saw any contradiction. It was not just that in practice a millowner was the best leader the workers could then hope for. A millowner who was a friend to his men, who was a great orator, who drew on a spiritual and literary tradition of rare richness, was exactly suited to the working-class unrest of the 1840s and 1860s. From Cobden in the 1840s to Joseph Chamberlain in the 1880s, it was second nature for manual workers to turn to businessmen to lead them against aristocratic privilege and aristocratic government. Business had no historical vocation, no desire for power, on its own; its role, in Liberal eyes, was to speak for the people.

Never forget that Bright was a working businessman. His father's firm, started from nothing in 1809, and still going, was a success, but it did not run itself. Bright could never sit back and let the rents roll in, as could his opponents among the landed gentry. He had a business career, as well as a political one, and while being a historic figure on the national stage, he had commercial matters to worry about. He branched out into the manufacture of carpets, and had a sideline in the mining of lead and gold in Wales. This sense of having to earn his living made him remain further from the gentry than from his men, many of whom spoke to him on Christian-name terms.

The Rochdale background

Rochdale, like Bright himself, was a symbol. It stood for independence, manliness, progress, vitality. It had perhaps the most alert tradition of public discussion of any small town in England. On summer evenings, crowds gathered to argue the topics of the hour outside the Town Hall. It was Rochdale working men, the immortal Pioneers, who in 1844 founded the retail Co-operative Movement. It was a Rochdale Radical leader, Dr Kay, who organised the first system of government aid to primary schools in England. By the 1860s, 'Rochdale' summed up in one word the claims of the 'intelligent artisan', with his share of middle-class respectability, to be admitted to the political nation. Bright the individual can no more be separated from the context of his compact Lancashire town, than an ancient Athenian orator could be separated from Athens and its life.

Bright stayed true to Rochdale. He lived and died within a stone's throw of his mill. He, his parents, and both his wives lie buried in the Quaker burial ground there. He never had a rural retreat or a country estate: nor was there any flight to the leafy suburbs for him. He stood for town against country, in an age when country ruled the roost, and when the lines of division were sharp. That Bright's great political friend Richard Cobden, leader of the Anti-Corn Law League, was MP for Rochdale from 1859 to 1865, though having no direct connection with the town, only added to its prominence in national debate.

Cobden and Bright

Cobden and Bright are remembered, rightly, as an example of a great political friendship lasting from 1841 to 1865. Bright was not upset, but shattered, by Cobden's death in 1865. Where people sometimes err is in remembering them as the two leaders of the Anti-Corn Law League (1838–46).

Neither were among the eight founders of the League. Both, within months, had by force of personality assumed leading roles, but in different ways. Cobden was the clear national leader, the strategist, the master mind, in control of headquarters. Bright, at least between 1838 and his first wife's early death in 1841, was the League's man in

Rochdale, and one of its few leaders outside Manchester. Had Bright's first wife, the love of his life, not died, he probably would not have put himself heart and soul into national agitation, remaining at one remove from the centre of Anti-Corn Law politics in Manchester, only 10 miles away from Rochdale, but yet, as a great international metropolis, a world away from its small-town outlook.

On the platform, Bright and Cobden had different roles. Cobden was the reasoner, the persuader, the thoughtful student of the economy. Not for nothing had he begun his life as a commercial traveller. Bright was the passionate firebrand, the outraged moralist, and altogether the more emotional speaker. Bright was not Cobden's only helper, but, because of his domestic sorrows, he was much the most available for the life of an itinerant agitator, sleeping in a different town night after night. Other Leaguers were also prominent, either as speakers or organisers such as W. J. Fox, Colonel Thompson, Wilson, Ashworth, Milner Gibson, and Villiers. But by 1845 Bright had become indispensable on the platform.

It was not easy for Bright, as a widower with a small business, to take part in public life. His sister kept house for him and brought up the only child of his first marriage. His brother Thomas was indispensable in running the mill. Had his brother died, as he nearly did in 1843, Bright would have had no choice but to give up politics. When he became an MP, as he did for Durham City in 1843, he was even more rarely in his own bed.

Professor McCord's account of the Anti-Corn Law League[1] as a supremely efficient political machine, on a scale never before seen, need not be repeated here, for Bright was a campaigner, not a backroom organiser. He presented the Corn Law question as a working-class question, not just an issue concerning businessmen. He was eager to widen his attack on the landed class, for in his second parliamentary session (1845) he raised the Game Laws, another aspect of aristocratic privilege – the right of landlords to destroy their farmers' crops by keeping game for their sole use. As Bright argued, 5,000 poor men were convicted yearly so that 40,000 rich men could enjoy their sport.

Was Bright right?

Bright was undoubtedly totally sincere in his attacks on 'the heartless aristocracy of Britain' who trampled 'unpunished upon every right, human and divine'. He really believed what he said. He was also an ambitious young man, too much so for the taste of some of his staider colleagues in the League. He was right in thinking that there was exceptional distress among the poor, especially in 1842, one of the worst years of the century. He was wrong in thinking that this was especially due to the Corn Laws, rather than the general fluctuations of the trade cycle. Business has after all alternated between boom and slump for two centuries now. He was right on the narrower issue of Britain's growing need to import its main food, corn. He was wrong in thinking that campaigning by the League could by itself alter the political situation. A recent study by Professor Hamer[2] has shown how patchy, complex, and at times faltering were the League's methods and achievements. The Victorian myth of the League as the perfect pressure group no longer holds water, or only in a very roundabout way. As for it changing Peel's mind, Peel made his own decisions. As for Bright's emotional appeal, based as it was on the politics of hunger, it was misleading. Corn prices were moderate in the years before 1845, even falling. There was no famine. Harvests were good, at least until 1845. Food was not dear. As Gladstone said at the time, repeal of the Corn Laws would not create a general commercial utopia, as Bright implied, desirable though it might be on other grounds. Like most men who achieve something great, Bright had tunnel vision.

Strangely, as it now seems, and sadly, Cobden and Bright were among those who joined with Disraeli and their Protectionist opponents in throwing out Peel on the side issue of an Irish Coercion Bill in June 1846. With the Irish famine soon to gather full force, they removed the one statesman capable of relieving it.

Aftermath 1846-59

The Anti-Corn Law League was suspended in July 1846. For most Leaguers, it was time to return to their mills. For MPs like Cobden and Bright, it was a moment of false triumph. By removing a great sense of injustice, they had strengthened the aristocratic system. In the late 1840s, this was not clear. By the 1850s, it was. The mid-Victorian boom had arrived. Divisions between town and country, business and land, softened and narrowed. Radicalism lacked a new focus. In its place, nationalism excited the newly rich. With Lord Palmerston playing the part of John Bull, a prosperous country settled for a reactionary, bellicose liberalism, torpid at home and aggressive abroad. The new press of the later 1850s stirred middle-class emotion to unprecedented heights over the Crimean War (1854–56) and the Indian Mutiny (1857–58). It was not a good time to be a peace-loving, economical, reforming Radical. Bright's letters become filled with a bitter sense of betrayal. His own class, the manufacturers, had turned against him. Even in Manchester, home of the League, he was burnt in effigy because he opposed the Crimean War.[3] He was denounced as a friend of every country but his own, a man who thought of nothing but making money.

The consequence was shattering. Bright succumbed to a long nervous breakdown. He was out of politics from autumn 1855 to autumn 1858, losing his seat on the way in the 1857 election. Cobden, too, lost his seat in 1857, and when he returned in 1859 was fairly inactive in Parliament until his death in 1865. The 'Manchester School', it seemed, was well and truly over, rejected by its own kind.

Bright's comeback

Having largely lost the middle class, Bright turned to the working class. He built himself a second career as parliamentary reformer, and he did it without any League or political machine of his own. He did, however, have to bide his time. A premature reform campaign in 1858–59 fizzled out, though earning Bright much upper-class hatred; Lord Clarendon, a Whig foreign secretary, wrote of his 'almost unconquerable desire to give him a good thrashing'. In the prosperous years of Palmerston's second premiership (1859–65), Bright took things quietly, knowing there was little he could do. He did however broaden his range as a statesman, showing that he had a distinctively radical line on India, Ireland, and America. In America, the Civil War dominated English discussion. Most Englishmen, especially those in society, supported the slave-owning South, even at the risk of war with the North. Bright's outrage knew no bounds. It also, more important for the future, drew him into contact for the first time with the newly emerged national trade union leaders. Foreign policy, not parliamentary reform first broke the ice between Bright and the new working-class Radicalism.

Palmerston's death in 1865 brought a new Prime Minister, Lord Russell. Russell needed all the support he could get. Causing a sensation in London society, he even had Bright to dinner, the first step towards his acceptance by the Liberal leadership. During the complicated Reform crisis of 1866–67, Bright played a steadying role.

Reform crisis 1866–67

Outside Parliament, Bright was a figurehead, yet a successful and indispensable one. Nobody would now say, as his biographer Trevelyan does, that he won the working men the vote. The working men were already well organised, chiefly in the Reform League, but were unable to produce a speaker who looked like a historic leader. What Bright did not have was any control over the extra-parliamentary agitation. Never an organiser, in 1866–67 he was used by a great movement which he had not created.

Bright gave an intensely respectable tone to the cause of Reform. His speeches, full of uplift, and usually given indoors in the evening to an audience admitted by ticket only, exactly fitted the Reformers' theme of a serious, moral, and intelligent skilled working class which deserved to be rewarded with the vote. Bright was never a mob leader, had nothing to do with what scuffles took place in Hyde Park, and showed great skill in never putting a foot wrong at a time of great tension.

In Parliament, Bright was the main leader, though not the only one, of the left wing of the Liberal Party. Here, both in 1866 and in 1867, he was unsuccessful, in that Disraeli got the better of Bright's partnership with Gladstone. Bright wanted a Liberal bill passed by a united Liberal Party; he ended up with a Liberal government defeated in 1866, and a Liberal opposition cunningly split by Disraeli in 1867. In that sense, he did not get what he wanted over Reform. On the other hand, once Disraeli's bill had passed, Bright was the main beneficiary. The Whigs and Peelites, who had long and exclusively ruled the roost in the Liberal Party, knew that there was a price to be paid for the semi-democracy of the second Reform Bill, and that price was the admission of Bright to their inner counsels.

Bright as Liberal veteran

Bright was thrice cabinet minister: in 1868–70, in 1873–74, and in 1880–82. In 1868–70 he held a minor post, the Board of Trade, and thereafter held non-administrative offices. He passed no legislation of consequence. He was indeed unsuited to administration, of which he had no experience. In 1870 he had another breakdown, not speaking in public in that year, nor again until 1875, when he was a silver-haired remnant of his former self.

This is not the whole tale. He early convinced the party leaders that he was the safest of all possible Radicals. He became valued as a link with the populace, and a guarantee of honesty. Gladstone, in particular, took infinite pains to woo him, and to persuade him to re-enter the cabinet in 1873, to stay there in 1882, and to support Home Rule in 1886. Bright turned in the late 1860s, in the eyes of upper-class Liberal ministers, from being a great threat to being a great asset.

Behind the scenes, Bright played rather a larger role. He stood out, eccentrically it seemed to his colleagues, for the inclusion of a little peasant proprietorship in Ireland in Gladstone's Irish legislation of 1869–70. Today Ireland is a land of peasant proprietors. He also served as a link between the cabinet and religious dissent in their unending rows over education. Nevertheless, he was mainly a figurehead, as in the 1860s, but with a lower profile. What he did not do was perhaps more significant than what he did. He took little part in the great Gladstonian campaigns of 1876–78 over the Eastern Question, perhaps from jealousy of Gladstone taking his place as popular hero; and he came deeply to dislike Irish misconduct, going against them and Gladstone over Home Rule in 1886, his opposition, if not decisive, being well publicised. He left public office, however, not because of growing conservatism, but the reverse. As a Quaker, he could not accept Gladstone's invasion and bloody conquest of Egypt in 1882, and accordingly resigned – a man of principle to the last.

'In his later years, he found no great objects to pursue,' wrote his biographer Trevelyan, who saw the best years of his political life as closing when he entered cabinet, aged 57, in December 1868. 'He entered the cabinet and disappeared from the forefront of public life.' Even had his nervous health been better, he never showed any disposition to develop beyond the single role of orator. He never changed his mind on anything, holding in 1880 essentially the same views as in 1840, and he only once admitted to making a mistake, in having voted for the enfranchisement of women. If a static Liberal, he was none the less a thorough one, supporting the rights of Jews and atheists, opposing capital punishment and cruelty to West Indians. On the greatest of all his principles, his condemnation of 'aristocratic' war between nation states over questions of honour and prestige, he lost in his own time, perhaps to be vindicated in 1914. Unlike many provincial Radicals, he could operate effectively at national level, moving from one set of issues in the 1840s to another in the 1860s. As he said, 'My life is in my speeches.' The culture of a Quaker home and a small Lancashire mill town had given him all he needed to dominate an alien House of Commons and to reconstruct aristocratic politics. For Victorians, the idea of John Bright, the man of noble character and high principle, being one of themselves, was what mattered rather than what he actually did. And this idea legitimised not only popular liberalism, but liberal government. The Napoleon of Rochdale was the John the Baptist of Gladstonian Liberalism.

Notes

(1) McCord, N. *The Anti-Corn Law League 1838–46* (George Allen and Unwin, 1958).
(2) Hamer, D. A. *The Politics of Electoral Pressure* (Harvester, 1977).
(3) Taylor, A. J. P. 'John Bright and the Crimean War', in *Englishmen and Others*, 45–64 (Hamish Hamilton, 1956).

Further Reading

Ausubel, H. *John Bright: Victorian Reformer* (John Wiley, 1966).
Read, D. *Cobden and Bright: A Victorian Political Partnership* (Edward Arnold, 1967).
Robbins, K. *John Bright* (Routledge, 1969).
Trevelyan, G. M. *The Life of John Bright* (Constable, 1913).
Vincent, J. *The Formation of the British Liberal Party 1857–6* (Constable, 1966) pp. 195–244.
Walling, R. A. J. (ed.) *Diaries* (Cassell, 1930).

John Vincent is Professor of History at the University of Bristol.

Matt Cole
John Stuart Mill:
Architect of Liberalism

John Stuart Mill was one of the seminal thinkers of nineteenth-century Britain. Although his influence can be detected in liberalism, socialism and parliamentary reform, his career also illustrates the limitations of ideas as engines of history.

Mill's life and ideas

J. S. Mill was an extraordinary man in experience, character and influence. His father, radical philosopher James Mill, subjected him to an experimental upbringing based on the principles of his colleague, Jeremy Bentham, to stretch fully his son's intellect. John Stuart learned Greek at the age of three, Latin and arithmetic at eight, and political economy at twelve. He knew little recreation, and was isolated from children other than the siblings whom he taught. This 'unusual and remarkable' start to life, as he notes in the autobiography which it inspired, was a mixed blessing, but it left Mill with a spectacularly broad reading, a sharp analytical mind, and a conviction in the power of education for the improvement of both the individual and society.

In youth, Mill applied himself vigorously to contemporary controversies as a self-styled 'reformer of the world'. A devout Malthusian, he was arrested in 1824 for advocating birth control to London's poor; eagerly defended his ideas at the London Debating and Co-operative Societies; and wrote regularly for the radical *Westminster Review*. Influenced by the Romantic movement, he departed from the Benthamite utilitarians for the 'Coleridge' liberals and in 1826 suffered a severe mental crisis, depressed by the recognition that the satisfaction of short-term individual wants could not be the basis of justice as his father had taught. 'The whole foundation on which my life was constructed fell down', he wrote: 'I seemed to have nothing left to live for'. Mill emerged to reveal in reviews of Wordsworth, Carlyle and Tennyson his new faith that not all pleasures are of equal value, and that civilised society must cultivate attachment to the 'higher' pleasures.

The final formative influence on Mill's work began in 1830, when he first established 'the most valuable friendship of my life' with Harriet Taylor, the blue-stocking wife of a successful manufacturer. She moved in the same social circles as Mill, the Carlyles and Grotes, and quickly formed a dynamic intellectual partnership with him: a writer herself, Harriet contributed to Mill's work, most notably on women. Their mutual attraction was evidently more than cerebral, and despite being entirely respectful to Harriet's marriage, caused scandal. After John Taylor's death, they were married in 1851 to the delight of Mill, in whom customary cold logic was displaced by virtual veneration for 'the most admirable person I had ever met': upon her death in 1858, he wrote simply 'her memory is a religion to me'.

Mill's writings

Although his first major works appeared in the 1840s, Mill remained occupied by his career at the India Office, and it was after his retirement and bereavement that his most famous publications appeared. The first of these, *On Liberty* (1859), was dedicated to Harriet with the words 'it belongs to her as much as to me'. In it, he argues the classic liberal case for strict limits upon the power of collective bodies to interfere in our private lives. 'The object of this essay is to assert one very simple principle', he wrote: 'that the only purpose for which power can be rightfully exercised over any member of a civilised community, against his will, is to prevent harm to others'. Attempts to impose morality on private affairs – either by legislation or by the prejudices of Victorian public opinion – would only obstruct the path to individual fulfilment and general progress. *On Liberty* remains an outstanding vindication of freedom from censorship and tyranny over political or social activity.

Two years later, Mill turned to more specific constitutional matters in *Considerations on Representative Government*. Although a believer in the justice of democracy since youth, he had, on reading De Tocqueville's *Democracy in America*, begun to fear the threat to the common interest and individual rights posed by pure majoritarianism and a universal franchise. To prevent the feared bonfire of society's wealth and learning, Mill argued that non-taxpayers, the illiterate and the innumerate should not vote, and that educated citizens should be rewarded with multiple votes. 'No one but a fool', he said, 'feels offended by the acknowledgement that there are others whose opinion is entitled to a greater amount of consideration than his.' Voting was 'strictly a matter of duty' – to be done in the public interest, not that of the voter, and therefore accountably – in public.

Most radical of all were Mill's views on the liberation of women, which even he dared not publish until 1869 with *The Subjection of*

Women. He had always believed that no proof exists to establish absolute differences of ability between men and women, and his ideas had gained strength from discourse with Harriet. Mill condemned women's exclusion from professional careers and the franchise, their restricted education, and the scandal of domestic violence. The relationship between men and women was for him the last form of slavery, debasing both and wasting half the 'mass of mental faculties available for the higher service of humanity'. The 'natural' differences recognised by his contemporaries were to Mill no more than custom, but then custom was for many of his opponents the basis of society.

Mill and the Liberals

Mill took an active interest in practical questions, from intervening to save the trees in Piccadilly when it was widened, to muddying his hands in the waters of national politics. Throughout the 1860s, he funded working-class, liberal and radical Parliamentary candidates such as Gladstone, Beales and – most controversially – Bradlaugh; in 1863 he took the platform with Bright at a meeting of 3,000 trade unionists in support of the North in the American Civil War; and later he subscribed to the Reform Union and League (resolving the Hyde Park affair of July 1866 as the only figure respected by the authorities and militants) and helped found the Women's Suffrage Society.

Most directly, he took a seat in Parliament himself. Under increasing pressure from supporters, he consented in 1865 to be nominated: yet he declared that he had no personal wish to be an MP, would devote no time to local affairs, and – rejecting any appeal to voters' self-interest – would neither canvass nor spend anything on his campaign. His election for Westminster – the seat of Sir Francis Burdett and Charles Fox – was a boost to the morale of radicals within the emerging Liberal Party. Mill brought 'a wide and philosophical outlook to the problems of his day' and was 'a good Party man in Parliament', enjoying mutual admiration with the Liberal leadership. Gladstone's views in particular had converged with Mill's from the 1840s onwards: they met regularly, and the Liberal leader read early copies of Mill's books, attesting to him 'the sense of instruction to be gained from your writings'. The liberal concept of the 'active citizen', susceptible to improvement by education and political participation, central to Gladstone's Midlothian campaign, took nourishment from Mill's *Representative Government*. Mill reciprocated the respect of Gladstone, 'the statesman in whom the spirit of improvement was incarnate'. Gladstone's close associate Francis Lawley knew by 1867 that 'his impressionable and susceptible heart overflows with admiration for Mill', and opponents such as Cranborne saw him as 'the prisoner of Bright, Mill and Odger', conceding that 'any plan proposed and entertained by such a great thinker as Mr Mill deserved respect'. Mill was proposed by Disraeli as a member of the Commission of Enquiry into Reform of 1866.

Mill was thus a pioneer of liberal thought and action. Most importantly for progress by Darwin and others, he forged a bond between radical extra-Parliamentary movements and the Liberals at Westminster. As Maurice Cowling concludes, 'the (Reform) Union looked to Mill, Bright and Gladstone: so in 1866–67 did the League and the London Working Men's Association . . . They provided a link between the excluded classes and the inner sanctum of political power.' He was, to Vincent, 'part of the intellectual landscape of the self-educated from the 1840s onwards'.

Mill overrated?

Yet all this acclaim may overestimate the role of the lone J. S. Mill. Whilst loyal to Gladstone, he was a maverick member of the already crotchety radicals. His purpose in entering Parliament was to promote his own views, and he did so with an uncompromising rigour which baffled allies and enemies alike. He deliberately dilated upon his most unpopular ideas: at public meetings he broadcast his views on women, and reaffirmed to a crowd of workers his view that the working class were generally liars (to loud applause!). 'I was convinced', he wrote, 'that no numerous or influential proportion of any electoral body really wished to be represented by a person of my opinions', and one literary man in London society suggested that God himself could not be elected on such a platform. Mill could muster only 73 MPs to support his amendment to the Reform Bill granting limited women's voting rights, and alarmed Cobden by his demands for working-class representation, and Bright by talk of proportional representation. Other controversial moves included opposition to the Contagious Diseases Act, and a protracted campaign to bring Governor Eyre of Jamaica to trial for atrocities. Mill was derided as a remote, comical figure, from the pages of *Punch* and *Vanity Fair* to the speeches of Disraeli. The social awkwardness of his closeted youth afflicted him in age, and he was at times a poor orator, 'a book in breeches', as one critic put it. Even Gladstone said his speeches 'came physically as from a statue'.

It came as no surprise to Mill, then, when in 1868 he was narrowly ousted by the liberal Conservative W. H. Smith. Whilst some populist and Tory opinion – such as the *Daily Telegraph* – had supported him in 1865 in the hope that, in Vincent's words, he would 'ride the chariot of reform only to apply the brakes', they had been disappointed. He had even estranged cautious liberals – Bishop Thirlwell rued: ' ... if only he would have kept quiet, and not gone out of his way to give offence to his friends'.

Mill and parliamentary reform

No thorough analysis of 1867 can therefore give great weight to the role of the radicals, let alone one of their more independent and short-lived members. Even historians of the labour movement such as Dr Royden Harrison, who have highlighted the pressure brought by radicals, see it coming from the Reform League, rather than its tiny band of supporters in the Commons.[1] As Cowling says: 'One central decision was made, not by … Mill … and other leaders of the radical assault, but by a House of Commons in which the Radicals were a small, extreme group, reflecting neither the general body of opinion inside Parliament, nor the only centre of political equilibrium outside it'. Whilst Mill was respected by many, he was feared by few. Even his deepest admirers were restrained from giving him more than wistful reverence. Poignantly, Gladstone withdrew his name from a list of illustrious sponsors of a memorial to Mill in 1873 when the latter's views on birth control were publicised. It seems the price of public friendship with the stubborn and individualistic Mill was too high for any who sought power.

Life after Mill

If his influence during life was limited and indirect, can we claim any greater significance for Mill after death? Certainly the 'New Liberalism' of the turn of the century seems to owe much to the development of progressive thought pioneered by Mill, whose departure from strict Benthamism made possible state intervention alien to Gladstone, but reflected in Lloyd George. Mill advocated universal education, and in Parliament demanded subsidies for the Irish fishing industry. By 1911, the leading welfare liberal L. T. Hobhouse could say that 'in his single person he spans the interval between the old and the new liberalism' and 'his *Autobiography* remains perhaps the best summary statement of Liberal Socialism that we possess'.

The policies of the Asquith administration could indeed be identified with much of this later thought, but this coincidence does not denote causality. The driving forces behind the liberalism of Keynes and Beveridge can be rather more convincingly described in electoral or economic, rather than philosophical terms. Paul Adelman, for one, has refuted any relationship between, for example, Mill and Joseph Chamberlain's municipal 'good works' of the 1870s.[2]

Mill and Socialism

Some have even gone so far as to see Mill as the precursor of the broader British socialist movement. He had, after all, strenuously sought to design – and bring about – the means of fuller working-class representation in Parliament; he hailed Chartism as 'the victory of the vanquished' and deplored the poverty which 'chained the great majority ... to a place, to an occupation, and to conformity with the will of an employer'. The solution of co-operative production was one of his greatest enthusiasms, and as early as 1848 he wrote of socialists: 'On many points I agree with them, and on none do I feel towards them anything but respect.' In *Autobiography,* he stated explicitly that under Harriet's guidance, his 'ideal of ultimate improvement' had become one which 'would class us decidedly under the general designation of socialists'. Labour MP Mary Hamilton argued in 1933 that 'everything he cared for and stood for would, now, make him a socialist, not only in sympathy but in programme'.

Yet Mill's 'socialism' was partial, conditional, and a reaction to its time. He recalled battling *corps à corps* as a young man in debate with the Owenites; the first edition of *Political Economy* had dismissed socialist principles: and *Chapters on Socialism*, published in 1879, were at best an ambivalent appraisal, suggesting that many of the benefits of socialism (such as co-operative production) could be secured within a capitalist framework, and that socialists were dangerously optimistic about human nature. Mill despised the ignorant greed of Victorian capitalism far more than he relished the socialist vision, of which he had witnessed little. His commentaries concentrate heavily upon French socialism, and he appears to have been unfamiliar with Marx (not then available in English translation). The overt appeal to short-term class interest which characterised later socialist propaganda and action would certainly have run contrary to Mill's conception of the common good, and ignited his enduring fear of the 'Tyranny of the Majority'. Whilst he approved aspects of this 'ultimate ideal', it remained just that, for he was painfully aware of the constraints placed upon progress by the reality of an ill-informed and materialistic working class, whose demands for social reform he found to be no more than the desire for higher wages and less work 'for the sake of sensual indulgence'. Mill's rather Spartan socialism meant first and foremost that 'the rule that they who do not work shall not eat will be applied not to paupers only but impartially to all'.

A different democracy

If Mill's contribution to socialism is sometimes exaggerated, his relationship to the extension of the franchise is even further misread. It is often rightly observed that the very measures he advocated were carried through in the decades after his death, and that 'the question of votes for women' in D. G. Wright's opinion 'was not seriously raised until Mill made it part of his Westminster platform'.[3]

The expansion of the electorate, however, proceeded on a basis which would have been entirely disagreeable to Mill. Those granted the vote were not the learned or responsible, but those thought 'safe' by the authorities, 'deserving' (by virtue of some contribution to the nation as in the Great War) or merely those subject to the law. All are permitted to vote, none are recognised as superior to others, and, which is worst, the assumption is that the vote is to be used by the elector in his or her interest. With the Secret Ballot Act of 1872, Britain left behind the disgrace of open bribery and intimidation which had marred earlier elections, only to replace it with the familiar process of appeals to sectional interests of class or region from what Mill foresaw as 'base adventurers in the character of professional politicians'. In the privacy of the polling booth, he believed, the weak-willed and unsophisticated would use their votes for their own short-term gain and at the expense of other individuals and the community generally. Were he alive today to survey the desperate calculations of electoral strategists in the parties courting voters with offers of tax cuts and welfare bonanzas, his cherished idea of a democracy which would develop both the individual and society might be dashed.

Mill's influence, then, is arguable and largely posthumous. Where his ideas have been adopted, it has been for different reasons – and with different results – from those in his works. From earliest childhood, he was isolated from the everyday world: his vision of society and human development has been divorced from his paper constitutional proposals, like treasure robbed from a temple, by politicians who, for their own reasons, could not afford the rigour and originality of J. S. Mill.

Notes
(3) Harrison, R. *Before the Socialists: 1861–81*(Routledge and Kegan Paul, 1965).
(4) Adelman, P. *Victorian Radicalism* (Longman, 1984) p. 90.
(5) Wright, D. G. *Democracy & Reform 1815–85* (Longman, 1970) p. 106.

Further Reading
Cowling, M. *Disraeli, Gladstone and Revolution* (Cambridge University Press, 1967).
Mill, J. S. *Autobiography* (Oxford University Press, 1969).
Mill, J. S. *Three Essays* (Oxford University Press, 1975).
Mill, J. S. (ed. G. Williams) *On Politics and Society* (Fontana, 1976).
Vincent, J. *The Formation of the Liberal Party 1857–68* (Pelican, 1972).

Matt Cole teaches politics and history at Cadbury College, Birmingham.

Paul Smith
Ginger Beer or Champagne?
Palmerston as Prime Minister

Although popular in the country, Palmerston's premierships (1855–58, 1859–65) have often been seen as being characterised by resistance to reform and declining success in foreign policy. This view is now being challenged.

Lord Shaftesbury registered the extent to which the general election of 1857, more than any other of the nineteenth century, took on the character of a plebiscite on the Prime Minister. He commented:

> 'P's' popularity is wonderful - strange to say, the whole turns on his name. There seems to be no measure, no principle; no cry to influence men's minds and determine elections: it is simply, 'Were you, or were you not? Are you or are you not, for Palmerston?'

Defeated in a vote of censure on his China policy, Palmerston appealed to the country to support the manner in which he had vindicated the national honour when, as he characteristically put it, 'an insolent barbarian wielding power at Canton had violated the British flag' by arresting the crew of the Hong Kong vessel, *Arrow*, on suspicion of piracy. His smashing victory – a majority of some 80 seats, coupled with the defeat of the two sharpest Radical critics of high high-handed ways in foreign policy, Cobden and Bright – threw into relief the extraordinary contrast in the last decade of his life between his hold over the electorate and the distrust and dislike which he often inspired at the highest levels of society and politics. 'I fear he is not popular, except out of doors among the people; who say he is a true Englishman', Lady Cowper had written, with no doubt unconscious irony, when he was brought to the premiership in 1855, in order to stem the tide of failure in the Crimean War. He was then 70, and showing signs of wear, as Disraeli gleefully noted, describing him as:

> ... really an impostor, utterly exhausted, and at the best only ginger beer, and not champagne, and now an old painted pantaloon, very deaf, very blind, and with false teeth, which would fall out of his mouth when speaking, if he did not hesitate and halt so in his talk, here is a man which the country resolves to associate with energy, wisdom, and eloquence; and will until he has tried and failed.

Yet Palmerston did not fail; his domination of British politics in his ministries of 1855–58 and, more completely, 1859–65 caused endless frustration to those who hoped to replace him, not least the Conservative leaders, Derby and Disraeli.

The Debate

That domination, however, has often been seen as sterile, and Palmerston as a man who exploited the popularity conferred by a bluff, John Bull image and an acknowledged mastery in foreign affairs to hold up parliamentary reform and generally keep in check the more advanced liberalism which Gladstone's leadership was subsequently to liberate. The picture of a stationary and out-of-touch Whig aristocrat is neatly given in G.J. Goschen's account of how, in 1864, he sought the Prime Minister's advice on what he should say in seconding the Commons' address in reply to the Queen's speech of that year:

> [Palmerston] … ran through the various points of foreign policy that required to be touched … When he came to a stop as if he had finished his instructions. I asked him with becoming diffidence: 'What is to be said about domestic affairs and legislation?' 'Oh', he gaily replied, rubbing his hands with an air of comfortable satisfaction, 'there is really nothing to be done. We cannot go on adding to the Statute Book *ad infinitum*. Perhaps we may have a little law reform, or bankruptcy reform: but we cannot go on legislating for ever.'

In this reading, Palmerston barely sounds like a Liberal, and the attraction he exercised over conservative sentiment, to the great annoyance of the Conservative Party, seems all too natural. Yet there is a paradox about him, well captured by John Vincent, who, in surveying the emergence of the mid-nineteenth-century Liberal Party, recognises Palmerston as 'serious, intellectual, even theoretical; militantly progressive and humane; scientific and modern, to an extent rarely realised'; but all the same finds in him, if not 'the masterly architect of a policy of supineness', nonetheless one who was 'himself mastered by the supineness of the institutions and circumstances of the time'. Palmerston is seen as a genuine improver and reformer, who somehow failed, as Prime Minister, to do 'the work the age demanded', perhaps because he despaired of overcoming 'the resistances operating in the parliamentary system he knew', perhaps because he lacked sufficient popular support. Vincent's contention that he fell back on an uncreative system of parliamentary management based on 'crude belligerence abroad and class fear at home' receives a challenge, however, in the most recent study of Palmerston's premiership, by E.D. Steele. There we have a Palmerston carefully modulating his policies to the realities of international relations and to the state of domestic public opinion, dissipating class fear by proclaiming class cooperation, and offering through his governments 'a conscious introduction' to the era of democracy. The debate will continue as to whether his last 10 years should be seen as serving up the ginger beer of bluster abroad and stagnation at home or the champagne of a skilful defence of national security and class harmony, paving the way for a stable transition to democracy.

Foreign policy problems

Much of Palmerston's standing depended on the reputation for supreme ability in diplomacy built up during his great years as foreign secretary in 1830–41 and 1846–51. In his later years, with the resurgence of French ambitions under Napoleon III, the advance of Prussian power in Germany, and the growing strength (despite the Civil War) of the United States, there was less room for manoeuvre, and successes were harder to come by. Kenneth Morgan has suggested that it may not be too fanciful to see in Palmerston 'the first political leader who had to grapple, even in the mid-Victorian heyday, with the early premonitions of British national decline'. In 1850, he had carried off the blockade of Athens by a British fleet in order to defend the interests of (among others) that dubious character Don Pacifico, with the famous comparison of the British subject to the citizen of the Roman Empire, able wherever he might be to invoke protection by the claim 'civis romanus sum'. By 1864, when he was obliged to condone in the Commons the forcible boarding of the British ship *Saxon* by the Union navy, the Tory Lord John Manners was able to jibe that the house was 'assisting at the funeral rites and final interment of that celebrated historical personage, the *Civis Romanus*'. It was in the same year that the impossibility of fulfilling his near-pledge to safeguard the Danes against Prussian and Austrian attack in the Schleswig-Holstein dispute made crystal clear the limits of Palmerston's and Britain's ability to influence events in Europe, when sea power was of minor importance and no continental ally was available.

Palmerston's critics, who included not only pacifistic radicals like Cobden, but also Tories like Lord Robert Cecil (the future third Marquess of Salisbury), alleged that he compensated for failure to stand up to strong powers, like the USA or Prussia, by bullying the weak, like China, Brazil or Japan. His view of relations with non-European states, often in the context of the more or less forcible expansion of British trade, was certainly brusque. After the death of a British traveller in a dispute with a Japanese chieftain had led, in 1863, to a naval bombardment of Kagoshima and the death of over 1,400 Japanese civilians, he told Russell:

I am inclined to think our Relations with Japan are going through the usual and unavoidable stages of the Intercourse of strong and Civilised nations with weaker and less civilised ones. First – agreement for Trade, next Breach of Engagement, Injustice and outrage – The Redress demanded and refused – Then Reparation enforced by Hostility. Then temporary acquiescence – then renewed endeavours to break engagements – Then successful display of superior strength and then at last peaceful and settled commercial Intercourse advantageous to both Parties. We have gone through all these Stages with China – we have only got Halfway with Japan.

This sounds very much like Vincent's 'crude belligerence abroad', with a strong dash of European racial arrogance thrown in. The defence of Palmerston is that outlined by Steele, and has to do both with his view of international relations and with his understanding of what British public opinion wanted. First, the factor of power was paramount on the international scene: the weaker must inevitably bend before the stronger. Second, what Steele describes as 'the righteous and aggressive Protestant nationalism so powerful in the middle class and the unenfranchised' expected 'behaviour commensurate with being a Great Power'. At the same time, it looked for prestige on the cheap: expensive conflicts with major adversaries, disrupting commercial confidence and undermining social stability, were not good business. Palmerston's line was therefore to make the most of British strength where it could be successfully applied (generally through finance and seapower) and to proceed cautiously, even if demonstratively, where it could not.

Embodiment of national prejudices

Ministers, Palmerston asserted in 1857, were 'instruments of the national will'. How far he guided the public opinion to which he claimed to defer is an interesting question. His manipulation of the press was unblushing. Yet he often seemed content to follow rather than to lead, pandering to the complacent self-image of a free and prosperous England at the forefront of human progress, which his hearers liked to entertain. Dickens' Mr Podsnap, whose:

> ... world was not a very large one morally, no, nor even geographically; seeing that although his business was sustained upon commerce with other countries, he considered other countries, with that important reservation, a mistake, and of their manners and customs would conclusively observe, 'Not English!' when, PRESTO! with a flourish of the arm, and a flush of the face, they were swept away.

Mr Podsnap would have found little to disturb his self-satisfaction in the Palmerston who proclaimed Britain's primacy among the nations, and told a friend that it was 'unreasonable to expect honesty in a Portuguese or a Frenchman'.

His ability to share, or seem to share, the fundamental prejudices of a cocky and assertive nationalism - nicely symbolised by *Punch's* portrayal of him as a prizefighter - accounted for a good deal of Palmerston's popularity in the country; his appearance of being uniquely qualified to interpret public opinion to the House of Commons accounted for much of his hold on that assembly. How close to the public he really was is, however, a matter for argument. For Vincent, his appeal lay essentially to the middle classes. Yet he was no great admirer of them. 'He is a good fellow', he said of Richard Cobden, 'but extremely sensitive to attentions, being like all middle-class men who have raised themselves either by money making or by Talent very vain, under the semblance of not being so.'

If he held the middle classes in thrall, it was the result less of a real identity of feeling than of the appeal of his vigorous but prudent conduct of foreign policy, and of Gladstone's careful finance between 1859 and 1865, to the City and the commercial and manufacturing interests. No warmer was Palmerston's embrace of the working classes, especially when it came to the question of enlarging their political role. However he might feel obliged in his speeches to assume their attachment to the country's institutions, he feared that as voters they would be all too likely to be under the dictation of their unions or the pressure of their employers or the impulse of greed: 'Can it be expected', he asked in 1854, 'that men who murder their children to get £9 [death benefit] to be spent in drink will not sell their vote for whatever they can get for it?'

Palmerston and reform

On parliamentary reform, what Palmerston was prepared for, he told the Queen in 1857, was to enfranchise well-educated and independent middle-class men who happened to lack the current £10 borough household or 40 shilling county freehold qualification, and to let in some respectable working men by, say, giving votes to those earning a certain level of wages or having a certain sum in a savings bank over a given period. What he was not prepared for, he insisted to Russell, was anything which tended substantially to shift power from the aristocracy, the landowners and the gentry to the manufacturing, commercial and working classes. The bedrock of the social and constitutional system which ensured British stability, prosperity and happiness was for Palmerston the pre-ponderant influence exercised by the landed property of the country, whose privileges it was essential to defend. His idea of the natural order and working of British society was summed up in the image he invoked in the House of Commons of the charge of the cavalry at Balaclava:

> ... where the noblest and wealthiest of the land rode foremost, followed by heroic men from the lowest classes of the community, each rivalling the other in bravery, neither the peer who led not the trooper who followed being distinguished the one from the other. In that glorious band, there were the sons of the gentry of England; leading were the noblest of the land, and following were the representatives of the people of this country.

Such a view of society left small place for the sharing of political power with middle-class, still less working-class, aspirants. In this light, the willingness that Palmerston displayed in his last government to introduce middle-class ministers, like Milner Gibson, and to pursue a carefully guarded measure of parliamentary reform with the bill of 1860, can be seen, as it is by Vincent, as a notable earnest of the extent to which he was prepared to sacrifice his personal beliefs to preserve the unity of the still new and uneasy combination of Whigs, Peelites and Radicals that was now called the Liberal Party. Steele, however, makes a larger claim, regarding it as part of a conscious strategy to accustom the country to 'the idea of democracy, in a peculiarly British version'. Palmerston, in this view, was setting out, whatever his misgivings, to educate the nation for a new political future, largely by supplying in his speeches a rhetoric of class cohesion and common interest designed not so much to describe reality as to create an atmosphere of good feeling in which the transition to an enlarged electorate, when it could no longer be delayed, might be accomplished without the immediate dissolution of aristocratic government and of the social order which underpinned it. The element of confidence trick was perhaps no greater than all successful politics requires.

Conclusion

It remains that, if we credit Palmerston with a positive concern to ease, rather than just to delay, the coming of a more broadly based political system, and if we see his foreign policy as the controlled and measured expression, rather than the belligerent brandishing, of national pride and power, it is still hard to discern a vision rising above the day-to-day, pragmatic conduct of government at which Palmerston laboured so unceasingly. Commenting on the Prussian envoy's allegation, that Palmerston had no principle and no heart, the Duke of Argyll said:

> Palmerston was not in the ordinary meaning of the word an unprincipled politician. He was honest in his purposes and truthful in his

prosecution of them .... But what Bunsen meant was true – he had no ideals for the future of the world, and had a profound distrust of those who professed to be guided by such ideals.

For Palmerston, politics was about holding things together. Yet it was also, as he had shown at the Home Office in 1852–55, about humane and useful improvement, when that did not threaten the foundations of social and political stability. Palmerston was never totally negative or impervious to the hope of betterment. Florence Nightingale said of her staunch ally: 'Tho' he made a joke when asked to do the right thing, he always did it.'

Further Reading

Bourne, K. *Palmerston: the Early Years, 1781–1841* (Allen Lane, 1982).

Chamberlain, M.E. *Lord Palmerston* (GPC Books, 1987).

Krein, D.F. *The Last Palmerston Government* (Iowa State University Press, 1988).

Ridley, J. *Lord Palmerston* (Constable, 1990).

Southgate, D. *The Most English Minister ... The Policies and Politics of Palmerston* (Macmillan, 1966).

Steele, E.D. *Palmerston and Liberalism, 1855–65* (Cambridge University Press, 1991).

Vincent, J.R. *The Formation of the Liberal Party, 1857–68* (Penguin Ed., 1972).

Paul Smith is Professor of Modern History at the University of Southampton.

Paul Smith
'Leap in the Dark': The 1867 Reform Act

Gladstone's 1866 Reform Bill was defeated by a combination of Liberal Adullamites and Conservatives. Paul Smith explores how and why a far more sweeping bill came to be passed by the Conservatives the following year.

'Taking a leap in the dark' was a natural metaphor for Lord Derby to use about his government's passage of the 1867 Reform Act. First, it conveyed the fact that there was a sense in which ministers and MPs did not know what they were doing or where they might land. Reform, the alteration not only of the qualification to vote but of the arrangement of the constituencies and of the distribution of seats among them, involved such highly technical questions, and the statistics on which policy-makers relied were so imperfect, that nobody could easily tell how many voters different proposals would enfranchise and what difference Reform would make to the political system. Second, 'leaping in the dark' was a metaphor of the hunting field, which captured the element of trusting to luck as much as to a sure seat and safe hands that gripped a portion of the Conservative Party as Derby and Disraeli led it on what to many of its members seemed a risky gallop through an unknown country.

Two central questions suggest themselves. Why did a Conservative government pass in 1867 a much larger measure of Reform than its members had resisted from the hands of Russell and Gladstone in 1866? How did it get that measure through a House of Commons where it lacked a majority, where most of the m. ibers probably agreed with Gladstone that the bill's feature, household suffrage in boroughs, was 'beyond the wants and wishes of the time', and hardly any of them could have welcomed the great increase in electoral uncertainty and expense that the changes entailed?

We can adopt what might be called a 'macro' approach to these questions, seeking an explanation in terms of the overall social and political climate in which Reform was enacted, or a 'micro' approach, concentrating in detail on the small world of the governing élites at the centre of politics, and emphasising the part played by the imperatives of party advantage and personal ambition. Were Derby and Disraeli bowing to the winds of change, or simply 'dishing the Whigs'?

Great social forces

The two approaches have to be combined; the problem is in what proportions. To take the 'macro' perspective first, it is true that there were powerful forces in British society in the 1860s moving towards an extension of the political nation. It is sometimes argued that the victory of the 'democratic' North over the 'aristocratic' South which in 1865 closed the American Civil War gave a fillip to the demand for mass enfranchisement in Britain, just when many Radical and advanced Liberal politicians had become convinced that its growth in prosperity and respectability had rendered the skilled portion of the working classes worthy of admission to the privileges and responsibilities of full citizenship. When Gladstone, struggling to carry the Reform Bill of 1866, told the Commons, 'Time is on our side. The great social forces which move onwards in their might and majesty, and which the tumult of our debate does not for a moment impede or disturb ... are marshalled on our side', he expressed a feeling among reformers that they rode an irresistible tide. Yet how far matters moved in 1867 depended not simply on the existence of 'great social forces' but on the way in which individuals and groups understood those forces and sought to advance, exploit, or resist them. To explain the Reform Act, we have to look not only at the broad context, the macro level, but also at the micro level, where the party politicians made their calculations and sought their victories.

Pressure from below

It has been argued that what happened on the second level depended directly on the first. For Royden Harrison, the revolutionary potential of the mass agitation for Reform which emerged in 1866-67, against a background of trade depression and a cholera epidemic, especially as displayed in the Hyde Park riots of 23–25 July 1866 and the Reform League's defiance of the government in the demonstrations in the Park on 6 May 1867, compelled the politicians to undertake a large measure. He sees the timing and extent of Reform as determined by the fact that the British working class 'had attained precisely that level of development at which it was safe to concede its enfranchisement and dangerous to withhold it'. Subsequent studies have been sceptical of this view, finding no evidence that either the government or Parliament was intimidated or coerced by the pressure of agitation. The activity of the middle-class Reform Union and the working-class adherents of the Reform League, and the ability of John Bright in the latter half of 1866 to raise Reform demonstrations of over 100,000 people in towns like Birmingham, Glasgow, Leeds, and Manchester, certainly helped to persuade politicians of the desirability of settling the Reform question.

But that hardly explains why they passed a measure larger than the agitators expected to obtain and larger than some of their leaders really wanted — Bright for one was alarmed when household suffrage threatened the enfranchisement of the allegedly venal and disreputable stratum of the poor which he called the 'residuum'. The context of social forces undoubtedly pushed parliament towards Reform in 1866–67; but there was plenty of power of resistance and no loss of nerve among the political élites. To understand why they went as far as they did, we have to look at the play of party rivalries as examined in the outstanding analyses of these events by Maurice Cowling and F.B. Smith.

The Conservatives' position

The explanation in terms of party politics sees the Reform Act as the product of parties manoeuvring for advantage and using the Reform issue to try to attach to themselves the cause of safe constitutional progress or that of resistance to dangerous innovation, or preferably both at once. In relation to the Conservative Party, it concentrates on the efforts of Derby and Disraeli to regain the initiative and render the Conservatives a party of government after 20 years of minority in the House of Commons. Within Conservative politics, interest has centred on the role of Disraeli: was the 1867 act the result of the cynical opportunism of a man prepared to pass anything in order to win the parliamentary battle, or was it the conscious realisation of a long-held dream of establishing a 'Tory Democracy'?

To account for the action of the Conservatives, it is necessary to keep in mind their strategic needs, their immediate tactical position in 1866–67, the ideological dimension — how they were able to square what they were doing with their political principles, and finally the technical dimension — how their intentions were translated through the mechanism of parliamentary politics into the final act.

The overriding strategic consideration for the Conservatives was simple: how to get out of the minority position they had occupied since the party split over the repeal of the corn laws in 1846. That meant how to wrest from the hands of the Whigs the function of governing the nation in a sound conservative manner, with such occasional instalments of moderate 'progress' as the needs of the age and the temper of public opinion might seem to require. Between 1846 and 1866, the Conservatives were having a miserable time because that function was being performed quite adequately by their opponents. Palmerston was especially good at frustrating the Conservative Party by appearing to be the soundest conservative (small 'c') in the country, and after their disappointment in the 1865 general election — the fifth they had failed to win in 18 years — the Conservative leaders were reduced to waiting glumly for the moment when the energies of its Radical wing and the explosive potential of Gladstone should blow apart the coalition of forces under the Whig-Liberal banner which had denied them power for 20 years.

The tactical opportunity

What opened up all sorts of tactical possibilities was Palmerston's death in October 1865. Russell and Gladstone now sought a further demonstration that the Whigs and Liberals were the men to provide whatever carefully calculated advances might seem appropriate to the times by taking up the question of parliamentary reform. Russell, the veteran of the 1832 Act, had constantly used Reform as a talisman of Liberalism, introducing bills in 1852, 1854 and 1860. But if he, and advanced Liberals and Radicals, thought that they owned the question, many of their Whig and centrist Liberal colleagues were nervous about the changes in the balance of social and political power which it threatened. Reform in 1866 divided the coalition which had governed Britain since 1846.

This was Derby's and Disraeli's opportunity to escape the wearisome role of securing 'conservative' government by helping the Whigs to subdue the Liberal left. They knew that the Russell-Gladstone bill of 1866 was carefully devised to damage their interests through a partisan scheme of redistribution and county franchise arrangements which would undermine their strength in their traditional strongholds. They exploited the revolt of the Whig-Liberal dissidents known as the Adullamites to bring the government down, and formed, as in 1852 and 1858, a Conservative government in a minority (of about 70) in the House of Commons. What were they to do about the Reform issue, which the debates of 1866 and the popular agitation had pushed to the top of the political agenda, and the Queen wanted them to settle? Doing nothing meant waiting until the other side composed its differences, turned them out, passed a bill designed just as carefully as that of 1866 to damage Conservative prospects, and left them to face the next election as the party that had obstructed popular progress. Derby had been a stopgap Prime Minister before, until it had pleased the Whigs to eject him, and he did not intend to suffer the humiliation of 1859 again. It was he rather than Disraeli who decided to pursue the Reform question, though both could see the possible advantages of seizing the initiative for the Conservatives. If they were frustrated by their opponents in an attempt to find a moderate settlement of the Reform issue, they could appeal to the country as the defenders of safe constitutional progress against the Radicals. If they succeeded in putting the question to rest, they could establish their capacity for government and terminate the Whig monopoly of progressive legislation.

Disraeli had more than once openly announced his desire to break that monopoly. He and Derby had been careful never to commit themselves against Reform as such: they had even introduced a Reform Bill of their own in 1859. It was vital that they should not allow the country to think that a great internal question could be handled only by the Whigs. It was a major advantage to keep the details of Reform in the Conservatives' hands, so that franchise and redistribution could be adjusted to their needs. It was virtually certain that they could exploit the Reform issue to inflame the divisions of their opponents. There were solid, immediate tactical reasons for moving on Reform.

Tory Democracy

Was there anything more? In the mind of Disraeli who, since the 1830s, had urged the claim of the Conservatives to be the national and popular party, was there a vision of a 'Tory Democracy' which he saw the chance to realise? Modern scholarship generally thinks not. The Reform Act is not seen as stemming from a conviction on Disraeli's part that a vastly enlarged urban electorate would be Tory. For F.B. Smith and Lord Blake, Disraeli still thought in terms of the politics he had known all his life, in which Toryism was based on the landed and agricultural interest and largely resigned itself to the dominance of the Liberals in the urban, industrial world. As Blake puts it, he 'thought of politics as a matter of "management" and "influence" in the old-fashioned sense, not mass persuasion of a new class'.

The level of borough enfranchisement was relatively unimportant, so long as the county franchise and the redistribution of seats could be manipulated to protect the bases of Conservative electoral strength. Perhaps Disraeli was influenced by the not uncommon view that a borough franchise delving below the £7 rental line proposed in 1866 would bring in a class peculiarly open to Conservative influence. He was ready enough to discard the 1832 system, which he had always regarded as deliberately rigged to suit the Whigs by placing the boroughs in the hands of low, shopkeeping dissenters. But so far from being eager to implement some plan of Tory Democracy, he had at first been wary of introducing a Reform bill at all, and for Blake and others the extensive character of the final measure was the product of the technical problem of getting it through the House without a majority.

Disraeli preferred almost any concession to defeat. The bill had to be negotiated with various interests and currents of opinion in the Commons — though it will not do to follow Whiggish historiography in seeing it as a measure dictated to slippery Conservatives by vigilant Liberals. In the course of these transactions, Disraeli gave up all the counterpoises that had been built in to make the principle of household suffrage which was the central feature of the bill look safe.

The original bill was really as cautious as that of 1866, largely because the apparently sweeping proposal of votes for all borough household-ers was made to depend on personal payment of rates and thus to exclude the near half-a-million 'compounders' who paid rates through their landlords. This limitation was removed when Disraeli accepted Hodgkinson's famous amendment to abolish compounding in parlia-mentary boroughs, but it is not always noticed that he then promptly agreed to provisions which would have reduced the effect of that amendment by allowing compounding to continue on an optional basis. He and Derby had always wanted a moderate bill, but, weak-ened by the resignation of three cabinet ministers for whom even household suffrage with personal payment of rates went too far, and lacking a majority, they could not fully control the final shape of the measure.

The ideological dimension

Yet if Disraeli did not plan an urban Tory Democracy, he did possess a confidence in the cohesion of the British social system and in the capac-ity for popular leadership inherent in its upper classes which enabled him to envisage a large working-class electorate without great fear of the consequences. This raises a vital point in the ideological dimension of the explanation of the Reform Act. How did men of property, posi-tion and education in Parliament reconcile themselves to the creation of a working-class majority in a borough electorate enlarged by 138%? One answer is that, as long as the weight of the large towns in the rep-resentative system was not much increased, the amount of influence which the new voters concentrated in them could exercise was restricted. Another is suggested by Gertrude Himmelfarb's argument that it was mentally easier for Conservatives than for Liberals to accept Reform: Liberals, assuming a competitive, individualistic society, feared working men would mechanically employ their votes to pro-mote their class interests; Conservatives, with greater faith in the responsiveness of the masses to traditional authority, felt less terror of their impact on politics and society. This links with John Vincent's point that Disraeli was 'a Conservative social optimist, too sceptical to feel threatened or fearful as Liberal reactionaries certainly did'. But perhaps these views overstate the party distinction. A large measure of Reform was able to pass in 1867 because the facilitating rhetoric of social cohesion which Disraeli spoke helped many MPs and peers on both sides to believe that there was no catastrophic danger in large-scale working-class enfranchisement: traditional influences would continue to ensure the control of the established social élites.

Given their strategic needs, their tactical opportunity, and their pos-session, in common with many Liberals, of an outlook which allowed them to hope that Reform would be 'safe', one can understand why the Conservatives came to pass the act of 1867, and, given the technical problems of controlling its passage through the Commons, one can also see how that measure in the end went far beyond the one they had helped to defeat a year earlier, and far beyond the one Derby and Disraeli probably intended. F.B. Smith remarks of the bill that 'Ultimately it was shaped by chance'. But it was also shaped by partisanship. The Conservatives followed their leaders' adventurous riding and blind leaps because they enjoyed the exhilaration of seeing their Reform gamble exacerbate their opponents' divisions and disrupt Gladstone's hold on his party. That sporting instinct was illustrated in the words with which Disraeli was toasted when he was rapturously welcomed in the Carlton Club after a division which had demonstrated his ability to checkmate Gladstone's attacks: 'Here's to the man who rode the race, who took the time, who kept the time, and who did the trick.'

Further Reading

Blake, Lord *Disraeli* (Eyre and Spottiswoode, 1966).

Cowling, M. *1867. Disraeli, Gladstone and Revolution: the Passing of the Second Reform Bill* (Cambridge University Press, 1967).

Harrison, R. *Before the Socialists. Studies in Labour and Politics 1861-1881* (Routledge and Kegan Paul, 1965).

Himmelfarb, G. 'Politics and ideology: the reform act of 1867', in *Victorian Minds*, pp. 333–92 (Weidenfeld and Nicolson, 1968).

Smith, F.B. *The Making of the Second Reform Bill* (Cambridge University Press, 1966).

Stewart, R. *The Foundation of the Conservative Party 1830–1867* (Longman, 1978).

Vincent, J. *Disraeli* (Oxford University Press, 1990).

Walton, J.K. *The Second Reform Act* (Methuen, 1987).

Paul Smith is Professor of Modern History at the Univesity of Southampton.

Peter Neville
Examiner's Report

Peter Neville looks at the difficulties of writing essays on variegated movements such as Chartism.

Chartism is a central topic in British nineteenth-century political, economic and social history. According to the French historian, Edouard Dolleans, it was the movement of 'reaction of the working class against the Industrial Revolution'. His fellow countryman Halévy described it as 'the blind revolt of hunger' and the quotation underlines the importance of the economic and social issues addressed by the Chartist movement on which this question focuses.

Question

What working-class economic and social objectives found expression in the Chartist Movement?

Student's answer by 'Lynda'

Chartism was primarily an economic movement created by the depression of 1836–42, and yet there were also a large number of social reformers who joined the Chartist movement because of the desire for parliamentary reform which was common to both groups of people. Nevertheless it is clear that the economic and social aspects of the movement were the primary motives for the majority of the working class who did get involved, if only because support for Chartism can be seen to vary greatly and clearly between times of depression and times of prosperity.

The trade depression of 1842 saw the peak of Chartism, which then faded as the economy became more successful, only returning in 1847 when crop failures across Europe once again dramatically reduced the standard of living for the working classes. This variance in times of prosperity and depression is one of the few generalisations that one can make about Chartism. The diversity of its support means that there was little else that fully united its supporters.

A good introduction. A trap which many students might fall into here would be to ignore the political aspects of the question. The 'hidden agenda' is the political one which the question does not mention. But the Chartists were, of course, vitally concerned with political issues like universal suffrage and annual parliaments. Nevertheless, as Lynda has realised, the 'primary motives' behind the rise of Chartism were economic. But to achieve the redress of their economic grievances, the Chartists needed political power, and the 1832 Reform Act had failed to enfranchise the working class.

The objectives of Chartist groups varied greatly from area to area both because of inevitable regional differences and because, as with any working-class movement individual leaders and their ideas were extremely important in shaping Chartism in any specific area. The fact that Chartism was virtually wholly working-class also meant that communication between different groups was difficult, making regional differences even more marked. These regional differences showed themselves in many ways, such as the debate between those who believed moral force to be sufficient to instigate change, such as Lovett and his London supporters in the LWMA and those who believed that a working-class movement, since it has little political or financial power must, by necessity, use violence to achieve its end. It is, then, difficult to define the objectives of this Chartist movement, as the very existence of Chartism as a movement is debatable. Ward said: 'Chartism held an umbrella over a host of causes' highlighting the disparity of the objectives expressed within it.

One of the difficulties which Chartism experienced was that these disparate objectives were often not particularly complementary and were occasionally actually contradictory. It is even, perhaps, debatable whether parliamentary reform can be regarded as a unifying cause for Chartists. Although the gain of political power was common to all Chartists, the fact that each group wanted that power for a different reason meant that it was not an ideologically unifying aim, merely a practical one, since in fact it was an aim shared by any group which opposed the government.

Lynda rightly stresses the disparate nature of Chartism in this section of her essay, but then rather loses her way. One wonders why, for example, the section on moral force and physical force Chartists fails to mention Feargus O'Connor and identify the differences between him and Lovett. Something really needs to be said here about the economic downswings of the 1830s and 1840s which caused far more privation in the North than in the South. There was an obvious link between economic depression and the growth in Chartist support in the North. But the membership of the LWMA (printers, shoemakers, cabinet makers, tailors, etc.) was quite different from that of the Northern Chartists because these men were skilled craftsmen or artisans. They were the workers that F.C. Mather has called 'labour aristocrats' and their objectives were quite different too. The quote from Ward is apt, nice and short. Students sometimes think that littering essays with quotes from historians is an easy route to a high grade. But beware! Examiners are not impressed by essays which have lots of quotes (often memorised by heart, and not a real reflection of reading done) but very little argument or analysis.

Lynda flatters to deceive in this section, although she makes a good point about the links between a working-class movement with 'little political or financial power' and violence.

However, the disparity of objectives did not prevent Chartism from being a powerful instrument. The objectives of those who supported it were too important for this to be so. Although these separate groups had individual aims, nevertheless each was working towards this ideal. It is this new level of class-consciousness which makes Chartism clearly distinguishable from other parliamentary reform movements. Chartism was characterised by a broad range of objectives, both economic and social, and it is this which makes it so important in a historical context. Almost every working-class objective was represented by some faction of the Chartist movement.

Although the Charter itself was predominantly concerned with parliamentary reform, the main aim of the majority of Chartists was a reasonable standard of living. This objective was particularly one of the Anti-Poor Law Movement, and indeed many Chartist groups were formed in opposition to pieces of Whig legislation which were seen as damaging to the working class. The Poor Law Amendment Act of 1834 had angered many working men, and the APLM were the largest and possibly the most diverse of the groups. This was because the need for adequate food and shelter, particularly during the depression, was both the most pressing and the most widely acceptable of the Chartist claims. There was even some Tory support for the movement, as the issue was seen by many as a humanitarian rather than a political one. It was the need for this reform that began Chartism, and allowed many other political and social objectives to be expressed. The Ten Hours Movement was formed to oppose the Factories Act of 1833, and through this attempts were made to limit the exploitation particularly of adults in the factories. Although there were far-reaching implications to these ideas in terms of an employer's responsibility to his employees, it was nevertheless primarily an economic movement, much like the APLM attempting to improve conditions, particularly in the north of England.

In this section, Lynda correctly recognises the importance of Chartism as a means of working-class consciousness. But her judgement that Chartism was 'a powerful instrument' is questionable to say the least. The movement collapsed after all in fiasco and disgrace in 1848. There is a danger here that students may evaluate Chartism with the advantage of hindsight and not recognise its short-term failure. Lynda points out rightly how resentment against the 1834 Poor Law contributed towards the growth of Chartism (she could also have mentioned the Tolpuddle Martyrs case which caused outrage in the working class), but her claim that a reasonable standard of living was the main aim of the majority of Chartists needs qualification. Members of the LWMA were generally well-off artisans whose primary interest was in parliamentary reform and there were also middle-class Chartists whose objectives were quite different from those of working-class supporters. Indeed Sturge's 'Complete Suffrage Union' was an unsuccessful attempt to build a bridge between the Chartists and the Anti-Corn Law League, whose campaign against the Corn Laws was pre-eminently a middle-class cause. The link between Chartism and the Factory Act of 1833 is not made clear, and Lynda wrongly states that it was concerned with the treatment of adults in factories, when in fact its prime concern was to curb the use of child labour. This contributes to a feeling of confusion about this section.

It was, perhaps, the social reformers though that were of more ultimate significance. The Trade Unionists, and particularly Robert Owen, were to prove so increasingly in the future, since they were not primarily concerned with immediate economic conditions, but with the treatment and rights of working men at all times. This is the only Chartist group which can really be said to have prefigured socialism, as they had genuinely been campaigning for unskilled workers and were genuinely interested in long-term political gain rather than an end to short-term economic distress. The failure of the Trade Unions in this time is less understandable than that of the other major Chartist group, the anti-industrialists. Supported by many of the Chartist leaders, such as Cobbett and O'Connor, anti-industrialists wished to return to a pre-industrial Revolution country, when the standard of living of many working men had been higher. It is this objective, shared by a vast number of Chartists which to a certain extent accounts for their failure, since they could not have succeeded in this objective. However, it also caused difficulties because many had profited from industrialisation, and many were alienated from Chartism because of this movement.

Lynda begins this section by accurately describing the essential difference between the aims and objectives of Trade Unionism and Chartism. Care, however, needs to be taken about describing the Trade Unions as a 'Chartist group'. In fact, the Trade Unions and the Owenites were often opposed to Chartism because they wished to improve existing working conditions, whereas the Chartists opposed industrialisation altogether. Lynda says that the Owenites 'prefigured' socialism but it is important to remember that Chartist leaders like Bronterre O'Brien, Harney and Ernest Jones sympathised with socialist ideas. And the Owenites were not Chartists. There should have been a place here for Feargus O'Connor's Land Scheme, why it failed, and what O'Connor was try-

ing to do (remembering that the question focus is on 'economic and social objectives'). Lynda's reference to a 'higher standard of living' might be better replaced by a 'better quality of life'. Another point which this section of the essay does not bring out is that there was a clear difference between O'Connor's idea of an idyllic rural past, and the anger of Bradford woolcombers who had been put out of work by new technology. In this instance, the old technology was in revolt against the new. There was, for example, a link between the 'Plug Riots' (when workers in Yorkshire pulled out the new boiler plugs) and Chartist agitation. In this sense, Dolleans was right, but there was more to Chartism than just the 'blind revolt of hunger', or a revolt against industrialisation.

So, the main aims of Chartism were economic, yet there were some groups who were looking for permanent power for the working classes. The London Working Men's Association is an example of a more farsighted desire for parliamentary reform. The economic objectives were by their nature short-term. These movements were started as a reaction to the depression, and the immediate need for food and shelter. It was not these objectives that made Chartism so significant, it was the ideas of social reform which were given the ability for expression in the Chartist movement which were later to prove so significant. Ideas such as an employer's responsibility to his employees and the working man's right to buy newspapers as well as his more basic right to vote were all lasting and important. Chartism has been described as an economic movement which turned into a political one. This was mainly due to increased class consciousness, the very fact of working-class aims and objectives can be seen as a successful aim of Chartism.

The essay starts well and is generally well written. But it tends to stray away from defining what the 'economic and social objectives' of the working class expressed by Chartism were. Working-class Chartism was very disparate (Lovett, for example, being keenly interested in education while other Chartists were supporters of temperance, and women were encouraged to form Chartist groups) and Lynda recognises this, but its varied character and aims aren't quite brought out. Instead, other parallel movements, like the Ten Hours Movement and the Anti-Poor Law Movement are treated as if they were an intrinsic part of Chartism when they were not. On the credit side, Lynda has realised that Chartism was essentially an economic movement, but one which came to have political objectives as well. She needs too to bring out more clearly the striking regional differences in the Chartist movement, which were often a result of differing working-class circumstances.

Peter Neville is an A-level Examiner and teaches history at the University of Luton.

Index